MW01138767

.

BY TIFFANY JENKINS

High Achiever

A CLEAN MESS

A CLEAN MESS

A MEMOIR OF SOBRIETY AFTER

A LIFETIME OF BEING NUMB

TIFFANY JENKINS

HARMONY

New York

Harmony Books
An imprint of Random House
A division of Penguin Random House LLC
1745 Broadway, New York, NY 10019
HarmonyBooks.com | RandomHouseBooks.com
penguinrandomhouse.com

Copyright © 2025 by Tiffany Jenkins

Penguin Random House values and supports copyright. Copyright fuels creativity, encourages
diverse voices, promotes free speech, and creates a vibrant culture. Thank you for buying an
authorized edition of this book and for complying with copyright laws by not reproducing,
scanning, or distributing any part of it in any form without permission. You are supporting
writers and allowing Penguin Random House to continue to publish books for every reader.
Please note that no part of this book may be used or reproduced in any manner
for the purpose of training artificial intelligence technologies or systems.

HARMONY BOOKS is a registered trademark, and the Circle colophon is a
trademark of Penguin Random House LLC.

Library of Congress Cataloging-in-Publication Data
Names: Jenkins, Tiffany (Motivational speaker), author.
Title: A clean mess / Tiffany Jenkins.
Description: First edition. | New York, NY : Harmony, [2025]
Identifiers: LCCN 2024054287 (print) | LCCN 2024054288 (ebook) |
ISBN 9780593232637 (hardcover) | ISBN 9780593232644 (ebook)
Subjects: LCSH: Jenkins, Tiffany (Motivational speaker) | Recovering addicts—
United States—Biography. | Women comedians—United States—Biography.
Classification: LCC HV5805.J46 A3 2025 (print) | LCC HV5805.J46 (ebook) |
DDC 362.29092—dc23/eng/20241230
LC record available at https://lccn.loc.gov/2024054287
LC ebook record available at https://lccn.loc.gov/2024054288

Printed in the United States of America on acid-free paper

BOOK TEAM: Production editor: Cassie Gitkin • Managing editor: Allison Fox •
Production manager: Angela McNally • Copy editor: Alison Kerr Miller •
Proofreaders: Megha Jain, Katie Powers, Russell Powers

2 4 6 8 9 7 5 3 1

First Edition

Book design by Debbie Glasserman

The authorized representative in the EU for product safety and compliance is
Penguin Random House Ireland, Morrison Chambers, 32 Nassau Street, Dublin D02 YH68, Ireland.
https://eu-contact.penguin.ie

FOR ANYONE WHO IS STARTING OVER

AUTHOR'S NOTE

Just so you know, I have changed the names of some individuals in the book, as well as a lot of the details of their identities.

PART ONE

1

PRESENT DAY

A PIT FORMED IN MY STOMACH AS I STARED DOWN AT MY phone. I was backstage in Omaha, Nebraska, getting ready to do a show on the My Name Is Not Mom tour. Something about my husband's message was off.

"Hey babe, some of the guys here are making some stupid decisions. Not me. But I just wanted to let you know in case you heard it from some of the other wives."

In the nearly ten years we'd been married, this was the first text he'd ever sent that activated my Spidey-senses.

My heart thudded in my chest. The other wives he was referring to were my best friends. We'd all met in recovery when I'd first gotten clean and had remained close throughout the years. Our husbands were also in recovery and were also good friends. They were currently in Las Vegas on a bachelor trip for my best friend Amber's fiancé.

Colin and I met in early recovery and got married rather quickly. I trusted him with my whole heart, which is why I hadn't questioned the bachelor party plans. I knew he would do the right thing. So why was he being so weird?

I read the text over and over, trying to understand what he was referring to.

"Five minutes till showtime, ladies," Brent, our tour manager, called.

"Thank you," I mumbled, not looking up from the phone.

I knew they wouldn't be using drugs or drinking. Each of the guys had around a decade each of clean time, so that couldn't be it.

"Call me," I typed.

The dots to indicate he was typing never popped up.

"I have to go on stage in a few minutes, can you Facetime me real quick?"

My foot tapped impatiently as I waited for him to respond. Something fishy was going on, and I couldn't go out and perform without knowing what the hell it was. A terrible feeling crept over me, not just because I was worried about my husband, but because the men he referred to were married to people I cared very much about.

My mind raced. Maybe he meant they were spending too much money? That's probably what it was. I'd given Colin a budget for Vegas because if I hadn't, lord knows he wouldn't be able to control himself. Maybe the other guys didn't get one? If he could just call me I wouldn't have to speculate, damn it.

Deciding not to wait, I picked up my phone and called him. It rang and rang. No answer. He'd just texted me five seconds ago, so I knew he had his phone in his hand.

"HELLO?!?!?" I texted angrily.

No response.

"Is everything okay?" asked Marilyn, my friend who did the show with me.

"No, dude, I just got the weirdest text from Colin."

"Oh, shit—he's in Vegas, right?" she asked.

"Showtime, ladies!" Brent called, bursting through the door. I shook my head and stared at the text one last time.

I was angry that he would send a text like that right before my show and then not answer when I called. But more than angry, I was terrified about this feeling in my gut. Something bad was happening, and I had no clue what it was.

2

—

I COULDN'T EXIT THE STAGE FAST ENOUGH, DESPERATE TO
hear my husband's explanation. I didn't even acknowledge the se-
curity or staff on my way back to the dressing room like I usually
did. I'd spent the past two hours on stage, forcing the worries
down so I could make these people laugh, and all I wanted to do
was talk to my husband.

I picked up my phone and gasped . . . Not because I saw
something that shocked me, but because I didn't see anything. He
hadn't responded the entire time I was gone. My heart hammered
as I furiously texted, "What the fuck?"

What had he been doing for the past two hours? Why would
he send such an ominous message and then disappear?

"What did he say?" Marilyn asked, entering the greenroom.

"Nothing, dude, not a peep. It's so messed up—he knows I
had a show tonight and he knows I have horrible anxiety, so like
why would he send that and not elaborate? I'm actually furious

now." I looked down at my phone and realized my hands were shaking.

"We gotta go do the meet-and-greet. You gonna be okay?"

"I have a bad fucking feeling about this, dude. Something is off. Gimme just a sec. I'll be right out," I mumbled.

I called my mother-in-law to check on the kids, and hearing their voices made me feel better. But the fact that she hadn't heard from Colin once since we'd left four days ago pissed me off even more. A good dad would have checked in on his kids. A good husband would answer his wife's fucking calls.

Just then my phone rang. It was him.

"What the hell is going on? Why aren't you answering?"

"Sorry, babe, I was talking to the guys."

"Facetime me real quick," I said.

"I can't, I'm sorry. I'm at a football game."

"I don't give a shit. I just had to spend two hours on stage thinking the worst. I just need a little reassurance."

Click.

I pulled the phone away from my ear in disbelief. He'd hung up on me.

I called him on Facetime, my blood boiling. I needed to get out to the meet-and-greet, but more than anything, I needed to know why my husband was being so weird.

I let out a sigh of relief once he answered.

"What?!" he asked, annoyed.

"You can't send me a text like that and then disappear. My mind is friggin' racing, Colin. What is going on?"

"Nothing, just some guys making poor decisions. It's not really my business, I just wanted to give you a heads-up. Damn. Why are you freaking out?"

Did I imagine it, or did he just slur the word "out"? I studied his eyes to check his pupils, but I couldn't see them because of the bright stadium lights. I knew something was off.

I narrowed my eyes and bit the corner of my lip. "What kind of bad choices?"

"I don't know, babe, just . . . Fuck, dude, I really didn't want to rat anyone out." There it was again, that word. He'd definitely slurred it this time.

"Just tell me, dude. I gotta go do a meet-and-greet."

"Listen, I gotta go. We can talk about this later, okay? It's really none of my business, Tiffany, it's their shit. If I would have known you were gonna get this crazy over it I wouldn't have said anything."

"Crazy"?! I felt like I was being pretty damn composed considering the level of sketch my husband's behavior had reached. He was usually transparent about things, and as far as I'd known, incredibly honest with me. He'd never hesitated to tell me the truth, even if it hurt my feelings, so why was it so important to him to keep whatever the hell this was from me?

"I gotta go," he said, hanging up before I could respond.

Rage welled up inside me. The audacity of this asshole to turn this around on me and make me seem like the crazy one. I had asked a simple question.

Did I have a right to know? It felt like I did. But maybe he was right—maybe I should have just appreciated him giving me a heads-up instead of turning into a detective. I hated questioning myself like this. But something was off, and I was going to get to the bottom of it as soon as this meet-and-greet was over.

3

SMILE, SHAKE HANDS, HUG, ENGAGE, SEEM HAPPY, TAKE photos, say thank you, wave goodbye. We repeated this process over and over again until the line dwindled down to only a few people. I couldn't remember meeting anyone; I was too busy imagining what could possibly be happening in Vegas.

As we waved off the last of the people, I was informed it would be about twenty minutes until the crew was packed and ready to go. I marched straight to the greenroom, on a mission.

"Call me immediately and tell me everything or I'll tell the other women that something is going on."

I wasn't sure if a threat would work, but it was worth a shot. Frankly, I was angry that he was even putting me through this emotional roller coaster, so I really didn't give a shit if it pissed him off.

My phone rang instantly. Of course it did.

Marilyn entered the room slowly and I held up a finger to silence her as I answered the call.

ilyn stood still in the corner of the room, listening intently with her hand over her mouth in surprise.

"Colin," I said as a tear fell down my cheek, "tell me the truth. What did you do?"

"Oh my God, Tiffany, nothing," he groaned in annoyance.

I shook my head and wiped away a tear. "I'm not stupid, and I swear to God if you try to make me feel crazy one more time I'm gonna snap. I need you to tell me the truth—it's the only way this is gonna work. Because if I find out later that you lied, I'll never trust you again and we will be done."

"I didn't do anything, Tiffany, I'm telling the truth." He ran his hand through his hair in frustration.

I stared at him for a moment, studying his face. I knew instantly. I just knew. He was lying.

"What did you do?" I asked.

"Nothing," he persisted.

"Colin, this is your last chance to tell me the truth. Did you . . . did you fucking use? Just tell me, damn it."

I was surprised by the silence on the other end of the call. "Hello?"

He stared at me for a moment and let out a sigh. "I fucked up."

It hit me like a ton of bricks: Life as I knew it would never be the same.

4

2013

THE *DING* OF THE REGISTER OPENING CAUSED ME TO JUMP. I'd been staring down at the hotdogs spinning on the roller grill in awe, the way a new mom stares at her baby in the crib. Before that, I'd slowly strolled through the candy bar aisle, running my fingers across the smooth, colorful packaging as I passed. *I can't believe I'm here.*

A small part of me expected the SWAT team to burst through the door any moment to throw me to the ground and pull me away from this dream. This dream where I could spend three minutes looking at license plate keychains with names on them if I wanted. It all seemed too good to be true.

"Do you need help finding something?"

I spun on my heels to see a female employee standing behind me. "No, thank you, I'm good." I smiled, expecting her to continue on with whatever she was doing, but she didn't budge. I smiled again and nodded, reiterating that I was good, but she didn't move. Instead, she eyed me suspiciously, then glanced down at my purse. Suddenly it hit me . . .

"Oh my gosh! You think I'm stealing, don't you?" I accidentally yelled. She glanced around nervously, and I laughed. "Oh my goodness. This is so funny. Now that you mention it, I probably do look suspicious . . ."

"I didn't mention anything—"

"So, here's the thing: This is my first time in a convenience store by myself," I said as the woman shifted uncomfortably. "Well, not, like, ever . . . I've been in one before, obviously, but this is the first time in almost a year I've been allowed in one alone." I smiled.

The woman took a step back, and I knew this wasn't coming out the way I intended.

"No, I'm not, like, crazy or anything," I laughed, sounding crazy. "I've just been locked up for like a year and this is the first time since that I've been in a store unsupervised, and it's blowing my mind," I said excitedly. "We take this stuff for granted, you know?" I continued. "Like that guy over there." I pointed to a man in a business suit standing at the counter having a heated phone conversation with someone via his AirPods. "He's completely ignoring the cashier and being rude. He has no idea how lucky he is to have the freedom to purchase that salad without a corrections officer standing behind him and breathing down his neck."

I wanted to give another example, but the woman in front of me began to point at something past me. "I've gotta go," she said with a blank look on her face. "There's a delivery in the back and I—" She took off before finishing her sentence and power-walked away until she was out of sight. I think I freaked her out.

I saw the businessman leave the store without so much as a thank-you to the person who rang him up, and I shook my head. *We are so freakin' lucky and most of us don't realize it,* I thought. *I didn't realize it . . . not until all of this had been stripped away from me.*

On my way to the front of the store, the sight of a beer cooler to my right stopped me dead in my tracks. It felt illegal to be this close to alcohol. I surveyed the shelves and all the familiar labels on the bottles, and a lifetime of memories came flooding back. It used to be so fun to stop by this gas station and pick up beer and gossip with my girlfriends. I smiled, thinking about all the times I'd swung by after work and picked up a pack of Bud Light and sat around the fire with my friends until the early hours of the morning. In my mind these were lovely experiences, but my smile faded once the veil of these memories fell away, revealing the truth about what actually happened once I put alcohol in my system. The alcohol would turn to shooting pills into my veins in no time. I didn't have the ability to stop myself once I started; it didn't matter what it was. If it made me feel different, I would chase it like my life depended on it. I am an addict, and once I opened the cage, the monster inside me would ravage my life in no time. The hairs on my arms stood straight up on my skin and I shuddered. The thin piece of glass on the door of the cooler was the only thing separating me and my worst nightmare.

Yet here I was, walking away from the cooler and saying no. *I have a choice today and I choose not to give in to temptation. I've been blessed with a second chance and I sure as hell won't take it for granted.*

"Can I please have a pack of 305s," I said, pulling the four crumpled singles from my pocket. It was all the money I had to my name, and naturally I'd decided cigarettes take precedence over food.

"I was about to send a search team in for you," my dad joked as I sat down in the passenger seat.

"I know! I'm sorry, I didn't mean to take so long—it was just so crazy being in there unsupervised. I felt like a little kid whose parents left them home alone for the first time, you know?" I buckled my seatbelt.

"I think your mother and I went to a bar the first time we left you alone. Man, that was nice. Life really opened up for us once you hit thirteen," he said, pretending to reminisce.

I gave him a gentle punch on the arm and laughed. "For real though, Dad, do you know I haven't been by myself, unsupervised, in like a year? It felt so weird, like I was doing something wrong."

"Get used to it, kiddo, you're free now." He smiled, patting my leg. "You ready to go meet your new friends?"

My stomach did a somersault. He'd just picked me up from rehab and we were on our way to move me into the halfway house. I was terrified. I hated women and structure and rules, but I knew this was a necessary step if I wanted to stay clean. Which I did . . .

I thought.

"Yup, I'm ready," I lied. My heart fluttered in my chest once reality set in. In less than five minutes, my life was going to change completely.

5

―

"WELCOME TO NUSTEP! WE ARE SO HAPPY YOU'RE HERE!" The smiling stranger threw open her arms and walked toward me. I fought the urge to recoil from her. It had been a long time since I'd been able to touch another human, and somehow it felt incredibly foreign.

I looked over at my dad, who was stifling a laugh as this woman patted my back; it was like she was trying to burp me. "I'm Mary, I'm the house manager," she said as she pulled away. Mary had white hair pulled neatly into a clip and obnoxiously large bright red glasses that fit her boisterous personality perfectly. "You are going to love it here at NuStep. Follow me," she said, dancing into the house. This was a "faith-based sober living facility"—I doubted I was going to "love it." I still had some anger toward God, but I was willing to be open-minded for the sake of having a place to live.

"Is this weird?" I grumbled out of the side of my mouth as I followed her inside.

"I think she's hot," my dad replied. I laughed and gently punched him in the arm.

I nearly gasped as I entered the home.

When I envisioned a women's halfway house, I pictured a dark, cold building with dirty floors. Kind of like a traphouse, just fewer drugs and less sadness. This place looked like a model home. White couches, fresh flowers in vases, framed photos of smiling women adorning the walls, and the smell of apples and cinnamon wafting through the air.

"It smells delicious," I said. Mary stopped walking, and I nearly toppled over her.

"Yes! It's wonderful, isn't it? Angela is making mini apple pies to go with our ice cream tonight."

"Ice cream?"

"Yes! Every Sunday after the meeting we celebrate making it through another week without drugs. It's a nice way to come together, reset, and prepare for the week ahead," she said proudly.

"That's so cool," I replied, trying to sound interested.

I followed Mary from the living room down a long corridor with doors on either side of the hall.

"This is where you'll be staying," she said, giving a courtesy tap on a door to the right before opening it. "Your roommate is Liz, she's wonderful. About your age."

I peeked in and noticed clothes and toiletries spread throughout the room. The bed near the window was stripped down to the mattress, so I assumed that would be mine. I felt a pang of guilt. Liz had definitely gotten comfortable having the place to herself.

"There are four rooms total, and since I'm the manager I get my own room," she explained, scrunching up her face with giddiness. "But the other rooms have two beds each."

I let out a silent sigh of relief. There had been ten girls sleeping in one long room at the rehab I'd been living at for the past six months, and I'd had to wear earplugs each night to drown out the symphony of snores and sleep-farts. This was a nice change of pace.

"Let's head to the kitchen and I'll go over some of the rules and then we can fill out some paperwork."

I looked up at my dad and smiled, and he gave me a reassuring shoulder squeeze as we followed Mary. My heart was starting to sink, though. I'd have to tell her I didn't have the money to move in, then find a way to convince her I would be able to pay soon.

I had gone directly from jail to rehab, and hadn't been working, so clearly I didn't have the money to pay rent. How they expected addicts fresh out of programs to afford a place like this was beyond me. It almost felt as if we were set up for failure. So many of us end up back on the streets after jail because we can't afford sober living. I couldn't go back to the streets—I'd be dead within a week.

We took our seats at the round oak table in the dining room. I glanced over to the kitchen and smiled, noting the cabinet doors were each painted a different color, giving the kitchen a bright, funky vibe. Suddenly a woman appeared from the dark hallway directly behind Mary's seat, her slippers shuffling against the floor as she entered the kitchen. She had dark hair tied in a messy bun and was wearing polka-dot pajama pants and an oversize T-shirt. My mouth watered as I watched her pull a diet soda from the fridge and pop it open.

"We can drink soda here?" I blurted.

Mary laughed and nodded. "Yes, of course."

I hadn't tasted soda in around six months because we weren't allowed to drink them at rehab. Felicity, the owner, believed the sweetener in the soda rewarded the same part of our brains as drugs.

"Okay, let's go over a few things." She flipped her packet to the first page. "Rent is one hundred and twenty-five dollars per week, and it's due Fridays. Since it's a Sunday, I've pro-rated the weekend for you, so we just did a hundred for this week."

I exhaled nervously, unsure of how to explain that I needed her to let me live there for free until I could get back on my feet. "Here's the thing, Mary . . ." I began. "Times are tough and I'm not sure I have the exact funds at the moment, per se . . . However, if you give me a few—"

To my surprise, Mary laughed. My eyes darted around, looking for what was funny.

"You didn't tell her?" she asked, looking at my father.

I turned to face him, and noticed he was staring across the room, trying to avoid my gaze. "Tell me what?" I asked him. Dad didn't answer. Panic rose inside me. "Tell me what?" I repeated, more frantically this time. "Dad?"

My father slowly turned to face me and forced a smile. I noticed his eyes were glistening from the tears beginning to form. My mouth hung open slightly as I attempted to process what could be causing him to become emotional.

"Dad, what's going on?"

6

"YOUR FATHER HAS ALREADY PAID YOUR FIRST TWO WEEKS for you," Mary said, breaking the silence.

"What?!" I yelled. Mary nodded. "What the heck, Dad. Why did you do that?"

"I don't know what you're talking about," he said, pretending to be clueless and wiping away a tear.

"Seriously, Dad. Thank you, but I can't let you do that. That's basically your whole monthly paycheck." I turned back to Mary. "I'm so sorry, but can you please return the money to him. I'll find another way . . ."

"There is no other way," he interjected softly. "You aren't exactly rolling in dough at the moment, honey. Plus, I know you'll pay me back. It's all good. Truly."

I turned to face Mary and gave an exasperated sigh. My dad was on disability, and I knew damn well this would leave him with next to nothing.

Mary gently tapped my hand and winked. "Don't worry, we

will make sure neither of you goes without. Now thank your dad and let's get on with the rules."

I felt like I could cry myself; I didn't know what to say. "Dad," I began, but he held his finger up to his lips and shushed me, pointing to Mary. I smiled and nodded, and turned back to Mary to listen to the rules.

"Curfew is midnight, and you must attend at least one meeting per day. You'll need to seek employment immediately, and until you've acquired a job, you must be out of bed by nine a.m.

"No fraternizing, no relationships, no drugs—obviously . . ."

I listened and nodded as she finished going over the rules. They seemed easy enough. At least I thought. I still couldn't grasp the idea of being out in the world alone. The prospect was terrifying.

I entered my new room with my dad following closely behind and tossed my bag onto the bed and frowned. After twenty-eight years of life, every single thing I possessed fit into a tiny kitchen trash bag. I always thought by this time I'd have a house, a family, a good job, and a good life. Instead I owned maybe four outfits, some eyeliner, and a toothbrush. How the hell did I let things get this bad?

"Oh, cool! You got a TV in here," my dad suddenly exclaimed. "Are you gonna watch *Cops*? See some of your old friends? That'll be nice," he joked.

I laughed and rolled my eyes, then shook my head in disbelief. I couldn't remember the last time I watched television. "Thank you for helping me," I said, feeling consumed with a sudden gratitude. For the first time in our lives, my dad and I were getting to know each other. We were both addicts, and the majority of our memories were blurred by the substances running rampant in

"Hey," I said, removing my shoes and crossing my legs on the couch.

"Hey," he mumbled.

"All right, I'm done playing. I need you to tell me what's going on before I have a damn heart attack."

"I don't know why you're being so dramat—"

"Just fucking tell me!" I screamed as the last strand of sanity snapped.

"It's drugs!" he screamed back. My blood turned ice cold. "It's drugs, dude," he said, quieter this time. "Some of the guys fucked up, Tiffany. John brought drugs on the plane, and as soon as it landed, everyone—well, almost everyone—started shooting them up and snorting them and shit. It was the craziest thing I'd ever seen."

Tears formed in my eyes, and I realized that regardless of who he was referring to, people I cared about very much were soon going to have their lives changed forever.

"Are you shitting me?" I asked in disbelief. All of the men there were in long-term recovery. "Which of the guys used?"

"It doesn't matter, I'm not gonna say."

"You better tell me immediately," I snarled into the phone, shaking uncontrollably.

"No, dude, I'm drawing the line there. This is between them and their wives. It isn't our place to get involved."

"So you're protecting these fucking scumbags." I shook my head. He didn't reply. "You didn't do anything, right?" I asked.

"No, dude, of course not. They all went out—" He kept talking, but I got stuck on the way he said "out." It was the third time he'd said it, and the third time I'd noticed a slur in his voice. Mar-

our systems. I'd been in jail when my father informed me that he'd been diagnosed with cancer and had quit drinking and using drugs. He was the first visitor I'd had, and the first person to say they loved and believed in me after my arrest. If he hadn't come that day and breathed new life into me, I wouldn't be here today.

With a sudden burst of appreciation, I leaped from the bed and wrapped my arms around him.

"Careful there, I'm walking with a cane, you know," he laughed, putting his arms around me. "I'm really proud of you, kiddo," he said. "This is gonna be really good for you, and I'm right down the road, so if you need anything, or if you feel like you wanna . . . do anything crazy or anything . . . call me. Please."

I nodded and wiped a tear from my cheek. "I will, Dad, I promise. I think it's gonna be good too. I won't do anything crazy, unless it involves ice cream and mini pies—"

"Oh yeah, are family members invited to these things? Like a two-for-one situation?" he joked.

I laughed and shook my head. "Let's go get ice cream this week, my treat," I said, opening the front door to let him out.

"You don't have a job," he laughed.

"Shit, that's right. Your treat, then."

"Deal." He smiled, giving me one more hug before he left.

As the door shut behind him, it hit me. For the first time in nearly a year . . . *I was all alone.*

Except I wasn't, because there was a stranger in my room.

7

"OBVIOUSLY THAT'S YOUR BED," LIZ SAID, POINTING TO THE twin-size bed at the far end of the room. "There's sheets and stuff in that hall closet. I was gonna be nice and make it for you, but then I decided I was too lazy."

I chuckled, lowering myself onto the bare bed. "It's all good. I actually prefer no sheets or pillows when I sleep." Her face scrunched up in disgust. "I'm just kidding."

"Whew, thank goodness. I mean, I try not to judge, but that would be weird."

"Hey, by the way," I said, "I'm sorry for crashing your room like this, I'm sure you were bummed to hear you wouldn't have it to yourself anymore, so I'm sorry."

"You just apologized twice in one sentence," she said, twisting her blond hair into a side braid.

"Oh, shit, I'm sorry."

"That's three!" she laughed. "You must be a people-pleaser. I used to be one too. Somewhere along the line I just . . . stopped

giving a shit what people thought about me. Anyway, I'm glad
you're here, and technically I only had the room to myself for like
a day. The girl in here before you got kicked out two nights ago."

"Oh . . . drugs?" I assumed.

"Yes. Well, and theft. She stole three hundred dollars from
Toni's purse while she was sleeping."

"Toni?" I asked.

"One of the other girls who lives here. Anyway, I guess Toni's
roommate was actually awake when Anna—the thief—crept in,
and watched her take it," she whispered. "Long story short, Anna
got confronted and kicked out and now you're here. Yay!"

I sensed a hint of sarcasm, but I also got the feeling that's just
how she was. Blunt and chatty.

"Yeah, I'm really happy to be here. But I'm kind of nervous.
I'm not really good at social situations, and I'm assuming I'll have
to meet everyone at some point tonight. It makes me sweat just
thinking about it," I said, fanning my face.

Her eyes lit up. "Don't stress, everyone here is pretty cool. You
want me to give you the four-one-one on everyone here so you're
prepared?"

"Umm . . . No, that's okay. I think—"

"I'm gonna tell you anyway. C'mon," she interrupted. She sat
down cross-legged at the edge of her bed, practically vibrating
from excitement.

I listened to her describe the others.

There was Mary, who I'd met. Then Tabitha, who was either
sixty or eighty and crotchety. She worked at the Goodwill and
wouldn't let anyone use her friends and family discount. Then
there was Toni, a lovable thirty-something who was a recovery
rock star and had multiple years of clean time.

"Really?" I interrupted. "Why does she still live here if she's been clean for years?"

"She was in prison for a few years. I think she counts that as her clean time."

Liz then described Sam, who she said was gay and would probably try to hit on me. I didn't care. I was mostly interested in men, but I was open to girls as well, as long they treated me well. Not that it mattered. Dating was the furthest thing from my mind.

"Oh, Alannah . . ." Liz said, making a disgusted face.

"You don't like her?" I guessed.

"She's new, and I'm ninety-eight percent sure she's getting high, I just have no evidence. When you meet her tonight, look at her and tell me what you think. She's the one with red hair who weighs like ninety pounds."

Liz continued talking, but my thoughts were stuck on what she'd just said. She thought someone at NuStep was getting high. In this house . . . *where I lived.* If it was true, it meant that somewhere under this roof, someone had drugs coursing through their veins. I found myself suddenly and overwhelmingly . . . jealous. I rubbed the creases of my arms—where I used to inject—hoping the feeling would go away.

It didn't.

"And then there's me. I played volleyball my whole life, but I injured my leg my senior year of high school and was prescribed opiates for pain. Eventually, my prescription ran out and the doctor told me I no longer needed them. My addicted brain disagreed and . . . well, you know how it goes. Pills turn to heroin turns to crack and an eight-year meth addiction, and eventually you get charged with burglary of an unoccupied dwelling and blah, blah, blah."

A normal person would have been shocked about her casual demeanor, but her blunt delivery put me at ease. As an addict, I knew exactly what she meant and how quickly one thing does lead to another.

"It's crazy, because so many people start using because they have legitimate reasons, like a doctor handing you the pills and telling you that you need them," I said, watching her rub lotion between her hands before rubbing it on her legs. She was getting all dolled up for the meeting. I probably should have done the same, but I didn't have the energy to pull my hair up into a pony-tail. "And then you have me," I continued, "someone with invisible pain, the emotional kind, who takes the pills to feel better. Or feel nothing, which was my case. I just wanted to feel numb. And they worked . . . until they didn't."

"Yeah, for sure. What is your story, by the way?" she asked, slipping her Doc Martens on over her cat-themed socks.

"My story, it's long. I don't think we have time . . ."

"What! I just told you mine and everyone else's. You can't hold out on me!"

This was one of those moments when I wished I'd paid more attention during Boundaries class in rehab. I didn't want her to know that much about me, but I also didn't want her to feel like I was being rude by *not* telling her. Anytime I told someone my story they started looking at me differently, like they couldn't trust me.

"Seriously, I hate talking about this . . ." I hesitated.

"Why? Who cares? We all have a past. I slept with my step-dad's brother for crack once," she said nonchalantly.

I cackled. *That* caught me off guard.

"What?" she laughed. "You've never done that? I thought we all had . . ."

I continued to laugh, harder than I had in a while. I liked Liz. I wanted to tell her what happened with my ex-boyfriend and my arrest, but I just wasn't ready.

What I also wasn't ready for was a meeting we had to go to in twenty minutes. I wanted to stay here and rummage through Alannah's belongings until I found her drugs. I hadn't shaken the feeling of wanting to use since Liz told me about her. But since I had to meet with my new probation officer to be drug tested the day after tomorrow, that obviously wasn't an option.

But then I wouldn't get tested for *another* month . . . If I did the pills *after* my appointment, they'd definitely be out of my system in time.

8

"DUDE . . . THAT GIRL WAS DEFINITELY ON SOMETHING," I SAID to Liz on the trip home from the meeting. I'd opted to ride with Liz in her car as opposed to the house van with everybody else so that we could talk shit. I'd met Alannah at the meeting, and she appeared to weigh around sixty pounds, with jutting collarbones that looked like they could cut glass. Her knees knocked together when she walked, her skin was pale, and her teeth were yellow and decaying.

"I know, right?!" Liz replied. "I can't figure out how Mary doesn't see it."

"Wait . . . What if Mary is in on it? Like, she's using too? What if that's why Mary is so nice to her?" I was suddenly overcome with excitement. If Mary was getting high too, the likelihood of me getting kicked out was just reduced by 100 percent.

"No way, Mary isn't using. I know that much for sure. She has a heart condition," Liz said confidently.

I burst out laughing. "You're kidding, right?"

"What?" She took her eyes off the road momentarily to shoot me a quizzical look.

"Do you really think a heart condition will stop an addict from . . . Dude, my friend had a pig valve put in his heart and lost his eyesight due to a MRSA infection from using needles, and then I watched that idiot shoot toilet water and lemon juice into his neck."

"No . . . I know, I'm just saying. It's not even just that. Mary is an angel. I'd know if she was getting high, and I promise, she isn't."

"I don't know." I shrugged. "You'd think a house manager would have a good eye for people who are messing up, and that girl Alannah is clearly messing up."

Liz nodded and paused momentarily to process. "All I know is, if she is getting high, I'm gonna find out and get her ass removed. She's a danger to all of us who actually give a shit about our recovery," she snapped.

"For sure. It's super messed up," I replied, gazing out the window and formulating a plan to get close to Alannah before Captain Planet over there got her kicked out. The war brewing inside me between my addiction and my desire for a drug-free life was escalating, and to be honest, I wasn't sure the latter would be strong enough to win this fight.

We pulled up to the house, and when we entered I noticed a few women I hadn't met yet, setting out bowls and spoons.

"Welcome home, bitches," a girl I assumed to be Sam said, throwing up her arms. Sam had on gray sweatpants and a sleeveless white tank top, and her hair was slicked back into a ponytail, with the bottom half of her head shaved. Lots of gay girls in jail cut their hair that way, and for some reason I found it insanely attractive.

"You must be the new girl!" she announced, jogging toward me with her hand outstretched.

I shut the front door behind me and placed my hand in hers. "Tiffany," I said, smiling.

"I'm super stoked to have another roomie my age here," Sam said, then placed her hand beside her mouth to whisper, "It was starting to feel like a retirement home in here."

The dining room table was large enough to fit ten people and unfortunately shaped like a circle, so we all had to face each other.

"Another great week on the books, girls," Mary chimed, setting down her bowl of dessert and taking a seat at the table. I studied her face as she spoke, trying to see any indication that she might be getting high. "I'm very proud of you all. I know some of you met Tiffany, but I thought it would be nice to quickly go around the table and introduce ourselves. I'm sure you all remember your first night here and how scary it can be. I want her to know she isn't alone, and we are here for her."

I swallowed hard and forced a smile. "We don't have to, I'm sure they don't want . . ."

"Don't be silly . . . It's customary. Liz, why don't you start?"

My new roommate inhaled sharply and gave an annoyed smile. "Okay. Hi, I'm Liz, this is awkward because we already met but, uh . . . I have seven months clean." A few women clapped excitedly as she continued, "I've lived here for about two months, and I love it. You will too. I don't snore, so you don't have to worry about that. Sometimes I fart in my sleep, but they don't smell because I'm a vegetarian."

Ice cream flew from my mouth before I even knew it was happening, narrowly missing Tabitha, who shot me a disgusted look. "I'm sorry," I laughed, reaching for a paper towel.

"I'm just messing with you, I'm not a vegetarian . . ." Liz laughed. The girl next to her shook her head and rolled her eyes.

"I'm Toni," said another girl. "I've got three years clean. My drug of choice was meth. I have a beautiful daughter named Makayla." She paused, leaning to the side and pulling something from her back pocket. "Here . . . I'll show you." She swiped through her phone, then turned it around and held it up for me to see. "That's my baby, ain't she cute?" She beamed.

"She is cute, super cute," I said, pretending to care. It wasn't that I didn't like kids, I just didn't get that warm fuzzy feeling when I saw them.

"Toni has been fighting like a warrior to get Makayla back," Sam said with her mouth full.

"Sam!" Tabitha scolded.

"What? What did I do?" Sam shrugged.

"It's okay," Toni laughed. "It's not a secret. I lost custody of Makayla when she was one, and she's been in foster care since. I've submitted the final papers and just have to wait for the state to give me the green light, and she's mine."

"That's wonderful!" I exclaimed, genuinely meaning it this time. I didn't know much about the foster system or what losing custody of a child meant, but judging by the way she proudly displayed her daughter's photo, I imagined this was a huge blessing for her.

The women went around the table telling me about themselves, and I tried my hardest to seem interested. Don't get me wrong: It was inspiring to be surrounded by all these strong women in recovery, but it was just a lot to take in. I hadn't even had a chance to unpack my tiny bag yet.

It wasn't long before Mary dismissed us for the night and I gladly made my way back to my room. After unpacking I lay down and closed my eyes, but my mind raced. I had so much to do: get a job, find my new probation officer's office, pay my dad back, repair broken relationships, save money, buy food, and get a sponsor.

You know what sounded better than all that?

Saying fuck it and snorting ten pills at once. Then I wouldn't have to do a single thing. I wouldn't have to stress or worry or plan or wait . . . All I'd have to do was close my eyes and drift into the abyss of nothingness, freeing myself from any and all obligations. It would be so much easier, and the idea of not having to live out my broken life was almost too tempting to pass up.

But I couldn't do that. I had to get right. I had come so far, and honestly, messing up would leave me in a position where no one would ever trust me again. I'd have nowhere to go. This was my last chance. I couldn't screw it up. No matter what life threw at me, I had to do the right thing.

That was easy to say, not knowing just how giant of a curveball life was about to throw full-speed at my face.

9

THE FOLLOWING MORNING WHEN MY ALARM WENT OFF, I opened my eyes and immediately panicked. I'd forgotten where I was and it took a couple seconds for my brain to kick into gear. I let out a sigh of relief realizing I wasn't in jail, or in a room full of women at rehab.

Liz was already gone, and I had approximately thirty minutes to get dressed and out the door to look for a job. I needed to get up and get moving, but I felt paralyzed by a sense of dread. For the first time in a very long time, I was venturing into the real world alone, and I was terrified.

For as long as I can remember my mind was like a train with only three stops. Stop number one: getting money for drugs. Stop number two: getting drugs. Stop number three: getting high. The train was fixed to the rails and never veered off course. During the years I should have been learning to save money, file taxes, and pay bills, I was stuck on a train to nowhere. Now somehow my train was on a brand-new course to somewhere I'd never been, and I was the friggin' conductor.

I was afraid.

I have no clue what life as an adult looks like without drugs coursing through my veins.

I've never experienced the world as a sober person.

The idea of being out there on my own made the hair on the back of my neck stand up. Since my arrest, my schedule had been planned for me, starting with jail, and then rehab. We'd wake up in the morning and hit a meeting first thing, then we'd spend six hours in classes like Home Economics and Boundaries, then more meetings. It continued like this until bedtime, leaving little room to fantasize about escaping to do bad things. I didn't have to think, and more importantly, I wasn't responsible if one of the plans didn't work out.

Now I was expected to make choices and decisions based on what I thought was best, and the truth was, *I didn't have the slightest clue what was best.*

The house was quiet. Some people had probably left for work and those who hadn't were likely still asleep. I'd hoped to "bump into" Alannah this morning, but now I barely had enough time to get dressed, let alone convince a stranger to be my best friend and give me free drugs. I hadn't given up on the idea, but it would have to wait. Plus I had to meet with my new probation officer tomorrow, so even if I did score, I couldn't technically do them until after my appointment. Knowing me, if I'd gotten the pills right now, holding on to them for that long without doing them would be impossible.

· · ·

Thirty minutes later, the Florida sun was beating down on the black wool blazer I'd borrowed from a clothes closet back in rehab. I wanted to take it off, but I was afraid my pasty white arms might blind the driver of a passing car and cause an accident.

I could tell my cheeks were beet red, but I wasn't sure if it was because I was dressed for a winter business meeting on a hundred-degree day, or because I was painfully embarrassed to be standing there.

The people in the cars whizzing by probably wondered what poor life choices landed me here, waiting for a bus. I used to do that myself, look at the people at bus stops and make up stories about them. "He probably got a DUI for drunk driving and lost his license," or "She's probably on drugs and sold her car for crack."

Now I was one of those people.

A year ago I was cruising around in a beautiful black Nissan Ultima with a radio, a CD player, and air conditioning. I could go anywhere I wanted at the time. Life would be so much different if I'd chosen a path that didn't involve illegal activities. God, I'd give anything to go back and redo it. I'd give my right pinkie for a three-second blast of air conditioning.

The bus schedule was complicated. There were many different buses at many different times going many different directions, and I was supposed to somehow make my brain coordinate a route that got me where I needed to be. It made my head feel like it was going to explode, so I decided I'd just hop on and see where it took me.

A bus finally screeched and squealed to a stop in front of me. The air compressor let out a hiss and the front of the bus lowered so I could step on. I approached the driver and noticed a machine next to her seat, so I assumed that was where I was supposed to pay. I hurriedly pulled the crinkled dollar bill from my pocket and smoothed it against my leg. I noticed the bus driver roll her eyes in annoyance.

"Sorry, it's my first time," I said quickly, sliding the dollar bill into the machine. It sucked it in, buzzed, then pushed the bill back out. "Uh-oh," I said.

"Try again," the bus driver said impatiently. I glanced at the people on the bus and gave an apologetic look as I slid the bill in again. This time it was accepted.

"Woo!" I cheered, pumping a fist in the air.

"Have a seat," the driver snapped, apparently not sharing my excitement.

"Sorry," I repeated, before making my way to the back of the bus. It smelled like body odor and mildew. The bus lurched forward before I could find a seat, and I quickly grabbed on to the closest rail for dear life.

"Have a seat!" she yelled again, glaring at me through the rearview mirror.

"Girl . . . I'm trying," I said, clearly struggling to make my way to a seat. I noticed an old woman laughing at me and shaking her head.

I decided I officially hated the bus.

I got off at the stop in front of the local mall. I figured I'd have better luck there than anywhere else since there were multiple stores next to each other. The moment I pulled open the heavy metal door to the entrance, it became clear to me that times had drastically changed since I'd last set foot in this building. It looked completely different from what I remembered. The stores were brighter somehow, and I immediately noticed the clothes on the mannequins in the windows of the stores were . . . much smaller than I recalled.

Part of me felt embarrassed at the thought of working in the mall as a twenty-eight-year-old, especially since the majority of the shoppers appeared to be giggly teenagers. I thought by now I'd be an actress or at least working on my backup plan, which was to become a teacher. "That'll never happen now," I mumbled under my breath, making a sharp right into a clothing store. A neon pink sign out front read "Socially," and the music bumping inside made it seem like a fun place to work.

As I approached the counter, a girl no older than seventeen with a nose ring and long brown hair greeted me with a smile. "Hi! Can I help you?"

"Hello! Do you happen to have any applications?" I replied, using my best customer service voice.

"Um, I think so," she said hesitantly. "Let me check."

As she dug around beneath the counter I glanced around the store. I had only been here for thirty seconds and the loud techno music had begun to give me a headache. *I used to take ecstasy and dance with glowsticks for hours to this music. What the hell happened?*

I made eye contact with a bored-looking girl in the corner, smacking gum in her mouth and folding shirts. I gave her a friendly smile and she quickly turned away.

As I continued to survey the store, I noticed the shirts hanging on the far wall were missing half of the material, and much to my surprise, it seemed leggings had made a comeback. I was a huge fan of pants without buttons. I didn't like having to put my muffin-top into a chokehold every time I left the house.

"You can have a seat on one of those benches in the back if

you'd like. Let me know if you have any questions, 'kay?" She gave me an overly fake smile and handed me an application.

I let out a groan as I lowered myself onto the bench. It reminded me of when my grandfather used to drop himself down into his leather reclining chair. I used to mock the noise he made, and he'd laugh and shoo me away. Since when was I an audible sitter?

Maybe it was the techno music, but I was suddenly and unmistakably aware that I was not as young as I thought I was prior to entering this store. I looked over at the teen employee and realized that to her I was probably just another boring, unfunny middle-aged woman who accidentally stumbled into a store meant for young people. It felt like only yesterday I was her age, getting my nipples pierced and passing out in cow pastures after keg parties. Did I step into a time machine and wake up in an old woman's body? I still felt like a kid inside, but judging by the whispers and awkward looks the girls were giving me, I clearly wasn't.

My existential crisis would have to wait for the bus ride home. I had to fill out this application and leave here with a job.

NAME: Tiffany Johnson

ADDRESS: Shit. What was my address? I didn't even think to look before I left. I quickly jotted down my dad's address. It would probably be better this way anyway, just in case they looked it up. I didn't want them to know I was living at a halfway house, not yet anyway.

PREVIOUS JOB EXPERIENCE: This was going to be harder than I thought. I had plenty of jobs in the past, but there's a huge gap in my work history. How can I say, "Sorry I got fired for stealing from a coworker, then went to jail for other unrelated crimes and have been in rehab ever since" without making it sound bad . . . ?

I'll just skip that one.

REFERENCES: "Sorry, I've burned every bridge and have no one to put here who would have anything nice to say." *Shit . . .*

HAVE YOU EVER BEEN CONVICTED OF A FELONY? (A FELONY CONVICTION MIGHT NOT EXCLUDE YOU FROM CONSIDERATION): A lump began to form in my throat and I tried my hardest to not completely shut down.

We can do this. We are here for a reason, and all we can do is be honest. If it's meant to be, it will be.

Self-Sabotage Me was trying with all her might to shut this whole operation down.

Optimistic Me wasn't having it.

Jesus, I really need a sponsor so I can stop talking to myself.

HAVE YOU EVER BEEN CONVICTED OF A FELONY? (A FELONY CONVICTION MIGHT NOT EXCLUDE YOU FROM CONSIDERATION):

I signed the bottom of the application and stood up from the bench with a newfound determination and marched over to the counter. "Here you go." I smiled confidently, handing the girl the application. She began skimming it quickly with her eyes.

"Great, so I will just take this and . . . Oops. You left this blank," she said, pointing to the blank question.

"Hmmm . . . lemme just . . . lemme see." I squinted and reached for the paper. My vision was so bad, I couldn't see that far. I hadn't gotten an eye exam in years.

"Ah, yes, work history. Sorry about that . . ."

"And the one under it," she added. I had intentionally left them blank, hoping the grownup who interviewed me would ask and I could explain in person.

I narrowed my eyes and pursed my lips. "Are you sure?" I asked, grabbing the paper from her. "Oh my goodness, what is wrong with me. I think it's the . . . music." I spun my finger above my head, gesturing toward the speakers. "It's very fun, and loud, and I think maybe . . ."

"Oh, is it too loud for you? I'm sorry, ma'am. We get carried away in here sometimes."

"NO!" I yelled, much louder than I intended. "It's not too loud, I love loud music. You should hear my . . . sound system in my car. It's . . . so loud. Listen, I think I'm just gonna take this home with me and fill it out and bring it back if that's cool," I said, trying to keep my feet planted firmly so they wouldn't run me full-speed out the door.

"For sure, no problem. We aren't really hiring right now any-way, so there's no rush." She smiled and picked up a pair of pants and began to fold them.

I felt my right eye twitch. I wanted to snatch those pants and slap her across the face with them, but the last thing I needed was another embarrassing crime headline. I could see it now:

BORING MIDDLE-AGED WOMAN ASSAULTS COOL YOUNG TEEN

WITH A PAIR OF BLUE JEANS BEFORE FLEEING TO MACY'S

AND SPRAYING HERSELF WITH PERFUME TESTERS

"No problem, thank you so much for your time," I said through clenched teeth. I turned and exited the store in defeat and could have sworn I heard the girls laughing at me behind my back. It reminded me of my childhood, when I was painfully aware of how awkward and unattractive I was because everyone mocked me anytime I turned my back.

Those little girls are lucky they got the new version of me . . . The old me would've stolen every single one of those ugly shirts off the wall then robbed them for all the cash they had in their register . . . I thought to myself, trying to defuse some of the anger growing inside me. *She's lucky I'm a new person or I would have—*

"Tiffany?" a voice called, interrupting the fake argument I was having in my head. I turned quickly and recognized a girl I went to high school with. Stacy? Sarah?

"Charlotte," she said, pointing at herself.

I was close.

"Hey, Charlotte! Yes, from Mrs. Meehan's class, right?"

"Yes, holy cow, I haven't seen you in ages. How are you?" she asked, lifting her sunglasses from her eyes to the top of her head.

Not as good as you.

Her business professional attire and A-line haircut made her look like she was preparing to defend some celebrity in a televised DUI case.

"I'm great, really good. Just . . . doing some shopping on my lunch break," I lied.

"Me too! Where do you work?" she asked.

I gulped. "At an insurance company, doing . . . insurance stuff. It's boring." I laughed, waving my hand dismissively.

"Oh nice, which one? I work with a few in the area." She smiled, carefully moving a piece of straight blond hair behind her ear.

"Oh, cool!" I beamed, trying to keep the lie going. "State . . . Farm," I blurted.

"Great company. So funny, I never pictured you as an insurance person. I figured you'd be an actress or comedian by now. You were always so funny, I remember that." She smiled and her eyes pointed skyward, as if she were viewing a memory of me from long ago.

My smile fell slightly as I was hit with the invisible punch of sadness and regret. I, too, imagined myself living out my dreams and entertaining the world by now. That's where I'd be if not for that pesky opioid addiction. Addiction doesn't care what your plans are; once you open the door for it, it doesn't leave until all your hopes and dreams have been properly obliterated.

"Right?" I laughed, throwing up my hands. "Who would have thought. What about you? What are you up to these days?" I asked.

"Oh, I'm an attorney, and a mom. Which sometimes feels like the same thing. I'm pretty much having debates with whiny babies from sunup to sundown." She threw her head back and laughed at her own joke. I laughed too, despite wanting to punch her for having such a perfect life. Beautiful face, great job, kids, probably a smoking-hot husband. Ugh, if only I had kept hanging out with girls like her in high school instead of running off with the misfits, my life would probably be so different.

Her laugh died down and she glanced at her watch. "What about you, do you have any kids?"

"NO," I bellowed, a bit too aggressively. "I mean . . . not yet. One day . . . hopefully," I lied. I'd never met a kid that didn't seem like an exhausting handful. I'd never understood why people were so quick to pop out babies. Caring for another person twenty-four hours a day sounded like a nightmare.

"Yeah, they are *a lot*," she said, like she'd read my mind, "but totally worth the headache. Being a mom is the best thing I've ever done." She smiled, sighing proudly.

I swallowed the throw-up that had risen up into my throat. "Cool, yeah, that's awesome. Congratulations, on . . . having kids. And being an attorney and stuff. Listen, I have to go. Lots of paperwork back at the office, but it was super great seeing you," I said, flashing a smile.

"Oh my gosh, you too, Tiff. We should get together for a drink sometime." She suddenly began digging through her purse.

"Call me." She smiled, handing me a business card.

I nodded and we parted ways. *We should have a drink sometime,* I mocked. *Must be nice to just "have a drink" without ending up naked in a stranger's bed or crying in a ditch somewhere.*

I watched her walk away, thinking about how at one point our lives were completely in sync. Walking the halls of the same high school, giggling about boys and sending off college applications. Then a fork appeared in the road, and she went right and I went left. Her path led her to a life of luxury and beauty, and mine took me straight to the pits of hell.

So far, life on the outside sucked, and unfortunately for me . . . it was only day one.

10

—

"SO WHAT DID YOU DO WHEN SHE TOLD YOU THEY WEREN'T hiring after you tried to hand in the application?" Liz asked with wide-eyed anticipation.

I'd just filled her in on my awkward job application debacle. I'd told Mary I handed in seven job applications, but I told Liz the truth, which was that I gave up after just one.

"Well, the old me would have probably roundhouse-kicked her in the mouth and stole some earrings on my way out." She laughed, and I continued: "But the new me smiled and thanked her for her time. It's because they thought I was old and uncool, I know it. I could feel it. But honestly, why have me fill out an application when you know you aren't hiring?"

She held up her finger as if she'd just had an idea. "Or maybe they *are* hiring, but they're afraid you'll slip and fall, breaking your brittle old-lady bones, and end up suing them."

I laughed and tossed my pillow in her direction. I didn't want to throw it directly at her since we were just getting to know each other and I didn't want to risk pissing her off. Plus, the last time I used a pillow as a weapon it didn't end too well for me. But that's a story for another time.

I liked Liz, and felt fortunate that out of all the women in the house, I ended up with the coolest one. Not to say the other women weren't amazing in their own ways, but Liz and I just clicked.

"I just feel defeated . . ." I sighed.

"You've literally only filled out one application."

"Okay . . ." I said, holding up a hand in defense. "One was all it took. It was traumatizing. Seriously, it used to be so easy to get a job. I could bullshit my way through any interview. Now I have to confess my gun charges to a teenage manager in the middle of McDonald's."

Liz whipped her head around so fast I thought she pulled a muscle. "Gun charges?!"

Shit. I didn't mean to let that slip. Damn it, I really didn't want anyone in my new life knowing the details of my past.

"Yeah, it's a long story. Anyway, I'm gonna hit the sack I think—"

"Umm, no the hell you're not," she said, setting the clothes she'd just folded on the dresser and scurrying over to her bed like a nosy little squirrel. "You can't just *casually* mention gun charges and expect me to be like, 'Okay, have a good night's sleep, see you in the morning.' Girl . . . *what did you do?!*"

I cleared my throat. "Just promise you won't say anything to anyone, okay?"

"I promise," she said, holding up three fingers.

"Okay, I feel like that's from *The Hunger Games.* That's not even the right . . . It doesn't matter. So . . . long story short, I was addicted to drugs for like ten years, and at one point I got into a relationship with a cop and hid my addiction from him. I stole a bunch of stuff that belonged to him, including his guns and—"

"YOU STOLE A COP'S GUNS?!"

"Okay, let's . . . can you lower your voice please?!" I pleaded. "Geez Louise, I just asked you not to say anything to anyone and the first thing you do is inform everyone in a twelve-block radius."

"I'm sorry, dude, but that's wild. I was not expecting . . . What?! You stole . . . I have so many questions."

"Cool, we can have a Q-and-A some other time. I'm tired—"

"Did he arrest you?"

"No, our friends . . . his friends did." A jolt of guilt radiated through me. I tried not to think about the day of my arrest too much. It was horrible. Being arrested by people I'd known for years was heartbreakingly humiliating.

"Do you still talk to him?"

Another pang of guilt. I wanted more than anything to talk to him, to apologize for all the terrible things I'd done, but my old sponsor told me only to make amends if it wouldn't cause harm to myself or the other party. We definitely weren't past the point of causing harm. An apology from me at this point would go over like a lead balloon. Too much damage had been done. Also, it would be illegal for me to make amends, given the restraining order he'd taken out on me and all.

"Not yet." I exhaled. "I'd love to tell you more, but I'm super tired."

"Totally, thank you for sharing. I didn't mean to freak, it's just . . . It was a shock. I can't picture you doing those things."

People said this to me all the time, and it always made me

smile, until I remembered that part of my problem had always been that I'm really good at fooling people. My counselor at rehab once told me I could "sell snow to an Eskimo," right before she kicked me out. She'd meant it as an insult, but I took it as anything but . . . I was a master manipulator and could make anyone believe what I wanted them to believe. I had always used my powers for evil in the past, but now that I was clean, I was hoping I could somehow use them for good.

"Thank you for saying that. I can't believe I did those things either. I mean, I can, I was there, I definitely did them, it's just . . . I can't imagine being that desperate now," I said, snuggling into bed. "Anyway, I'm gonna hit the sack. Good night, Liz."

"Good night, Tiff," she said, clicking off the light.

That last part was actually a lie. I could definitely see myself doing those things now, but I'd managed to push the thoughts about Alannah and getting high to the back of my mind until tomorrow. Tomorrow was a very important day. My entire future rested on tomorrow's events, so I had to put my obsession on the back burner until I made it through the appointment.

But after that . . . it was fair game.

11

___

PROBATION OFFICE, 2ND FLOOR.

My stomach fluttered while the elevator carried me up to the second floor. I was overdressed for the occasion, but I planned to look for a job after this appointment.

This was the first time I was meeting my new probation officer. As I approached the second floor I felt like I might vomit. I had this irrational fear that somehow my drug test would come back positive and I'd be forced to return to jail. I hadn't done any drugs, of course, but I'd heard horror stories of false positives, as well as people tainting food with drugs to send someone they didn't like to jail. It's horrible, but it happens.

Jail was one of the most devastating experiences of my life, and I couldn't imagine having to walk through those doors again.

I hadn't done any drugs, but if the test came back positive, I wouldn't be able to convince them otherwise.

I pulled on the door with a placard labeled "Probation," but it didn't open. I pushed on the door this time, and it still didn't open. I twisted the knob and pulled again with all my might, only this time, there was no resistance. It swung open with such force, it nearly knocked me to the ground, and I let out a manly grunt as I attempted to catch my balance. That's when I felt the eyes on me.

Through the open door I could see a lobby filled with curious onlookers, probably wondering who the drunk lady flopping around in the hallway was.

"Hello," I said quietly, entering the room and closing the door softly behind me. Everyone reluctantly went back to what they'd been doing prior to my awkward entrance. I tiptoed past the rows of plastic chairs, attempting to appear extra quiet, as if it would make up for ripping the door off its hinges. A large, angry-looking woman with frizzy red hair and flushed cheeks was sitting behind the window, typing on her computer. "Hello," I said politely.

She didn't look up. I glanced around the room to see if anyone noticed, then returned my gaze to her. "I'm Tiffany John—"

"Do you have your form?" she demanded, swiveling in her chair and looking at my obviously empty hands.

"I . . . don't. What fo—"

"They're on the wall in the basket, grab one and fill it out." She returned to typing before I could respond. I located the basket, took a form, and began to fill it out. "Not here." Her bark startled me. "Have a seat."

"Oh, duh. Sorry, it's my first time here, so—"

She stood up and walked to the back of her office before I'd finished my sentence.

"Alrighty, then," I mumbled under my breath. I snatched the paper from the counter and took a seat in one of the hard plastic chairs. I smiled at a woman who I'd accidentally made eye contact with, and she smiled back.

The paperwork was the same at this office as what I'd filled out in Marion County, where I'd gone to jail and started probation. Name, address, and phone number.

DO YOU DRIVE A CAR? No

HAVE YOU BEEN ARRESTED SINCE YOUR LAST CHECK-IN? No

DO YOU HAVE ANY CHILDREN? No way. No

ARE YOU CURRENTLY EMPLOYED, IF SO, WHERE? No

ARE YOU MAKING A RESTITUTION PAYMENT TODAY?

I winced. I hadn't been able to pay a dime of the $2,000 restitution I owed Eliot and his family. The least I could do was pay for the valuables I'd stolen from them and pawned—many of which they'll never get back. I could barely afford a sandwich from the 7-Eleven down the street. The chances of them getting their money anytime soon were very low.

I shook my head as I thought back to the days I'd stood at the counter of the pawn shop sweaty, shaking, and desperate. I'd anxiously thrust the stolen treasure toward the cashier, silently praying he'd offer me enough money to buy a pill. It felt like looking back on someone else's memories, like it was a stranger in an alternate universe committing felonies to keep from feeling sick. I couldn't imagine doing those things today, but I also know that addiction is doing push-ups in the parking lot, waiting for a weak moment to pounce. It was a different version of myself doing those things, but she was still very much alive somewhere inside me, and I had too much at stake to forget that.

I quickly scribbled "No" and finished filling out the rest of the sheet.

After I'd been standing at the window for what felt like ten minutes, the woman finally looked up from her salad. I smiled. "I'm finished, would you like me to leave it here?"

"Yes."

She went back to stabbing pieces of lettuce with her fork, and I went back to my chair. I didn't necessarily expect the people here to be friendly, but even just a smidge of kindness would go a long way in a place like this.

I surveyed the walls of the room and noticed a familiar poster. It was meant to be a deterrent for people who use drugs and featured a timeline of mug shots from the same addict. It began with a normal-looking photo and ended with a photo of the same person, only now their face was shriveled and sunken in, covered in scabs from picking their skin. Apparently this is what happens when you become addicted to meth, and I recalled laughing at the poster when I'd seen it in my ex's police station, wondering how someone could let things get that bad.

I got it now.

I knew firsthand how insidious addiction can be. One minute you're having fun with your friend, snorting pills and dancing the night away, and the next thing you know you're stealing money from wallets and breaking into cars to support the habit. I had no idea how low things could get until I lived it.

"Johnson!"

I gasped and instinctively stood up straight. Anytime an officer yelled my last name in jail I was required to stand at attention; clearly my body hadn't realized we weren't there anymore.

The first thing I noticed about the woman was the gun on her hip, and the second thing I noticed was her smile. I couldn't believe she was actually smiling at me.

I followed her down a corridor and into a room on the left. As I entered the room, I gasped.

12

THERE WERE AT LEAST THIRTY STUFFED MICKEY MOUSE dolls on the floor, and the wall directly across from me had countless framed photos of various Disney characters posing with what seemed to be . . . my new probation officer, Detective Sealey.

"I know, it's a lot. Have a seat." She gestured to the chair in front of her desk. "All right, let's get to it. Can you briefly explain in your own words why you're on probation?"

I wasn't sure that what I had done could be explained *briefly,* but I decided to try my best: Addiction to painkillers for ten years, not as the result of an injury. Then stealing, pawning those things I stole, and arrest.

"I had a choice with my sentencing, and one of the choices involved rehab, and that's the one I picked, because I knew I needed help."

"What were the choices?" She popped a mint into her mouth.

I stared at the wall and noticed Goofy staring at me with his stupid mouth open. "I could have done four months in jail, three years' probation, and six months of drug rehabilitation . . . or six months in jail, three years' probation, and no rehab."

She looked up from her paper and our eyes met. "Wait, so you could have just done two extra months in jail and been free, but chose to do six additional months of rehabilitation?"

"Yes."

"Wild," she said, shaking her head and flipping to the next page.

"Is that . . . is that a bad thing or . . . ?" I wasn't sure if it was her question or Goofy making me nervous.

"No, no. Of course not. It's just wild. I probably would have gotten the hell out of Dodge if I were you. No, you made a good choice. A tough one, I'm sure."

"Not really. I knew right away, actually. When I was in jail, I would watch women get released and within days be back through those doors, charged with something else. I couldn't believe it the first time it happened, but then it kept happening over and over. I couldn't wrap my mind around having the opportunity to listen to music and breathe fresh air, then taking that opportunity and throwing it away. I swore to myself that if I ever got released from that place I'd never go back. Plus, my dad got sober while I was in jail, and I couldn't leave him hanging." I smiled, thinking about how proud I was of my father.

"How's your dad doing?"

"He's great, still sober and kicking cancer's butt."

"Oh, I'm so sorry to hear that," she said. There it was again—the pity. My annoyance was then punctuated by the sound of her voice. "You ready to pee?"

I jumped up and followed her to the bathroom, shooting Goofy a bird as we went. She handed me a cup.

"Do you need me to explain how to give a sample?"

"Nope, I'm a pro." I smiled, waiting for her to exit the bathroom and leave me to it. She didn't.

After about ten seconds she nodded toward the toilet and my smile dropped. "Oh, wait—are you not leaving?"

"Nope, not today anyway. I have to watch you give the urine sample, to ensure you haven't snuck fake pee or something in," she said matter-of-factly.

"Oh," I replied, reluctantly unbuttoning my pants and taking a seat. Detective Sealey watched me place the cup between my legs, and once she heard the urine falling into the cup she turned around and faced the wall. I don't know why she bothered, as she'd already seen my bare crotch. Once the stream of urine came to a halt, she turned back around and with a gloved hand grabbed the cup from me and exited. When I met her back in the hallway, I noticed my cup sitting on a paper towel on the counter. She was dipping a white stick into it and staring at her watch. I rocked back and forth onto my heels, trying my best not to look nervous about the results.

"Alrighty, let's take a look," she said, carefully pulling the strip from the cup and holding it up to the light. "Uh-oh," she said, squinting her eyes at the test and shaking her head. My heart did a flip in my chest as she set the test down and crossed her arms.

"What's wrong?" I asked, realizing my worst fears had come true. "What is it?!" I was on the verge of tears.

"Well, you tested positive."

My heart dropped to the floor as I realized my new life was over, just as soon as it began.

Before I could speak, she stepped closer to me and lowered her voice. "Positive for being awesome!"

I stared, expressionless.

"Sorry, I'm just messin' with you. You passed with flying colors," she laughed. My face twisted into a look of confused horror. "C'mon, it's your first day, I had to pick on you," she said, tossing my cup into the garbage.

What . . . the actual fuck? How did this person get a job as a probation officer?!

13

—

"WELCOME, EVERYONE, TO TUESDAY NIGHT CLEAN. I'M DEVON and I'm a grateful recovering addict."

"Hi, Devon," everyone replied in unison.

I leaned over to Liz. "I have something to tell you . . . about Alannah," I whispered.

She gasped. "Ohhhh . . . do tell."

"Apparently she isn't getting high." I paused, almost too embarrassed to continue. I had royally screwed up with Alannah. "I asked her if she did pills, and she told me the worst thing she's ever done is smoked weed," I whispered, looking over my shoulder to make sure no one was listening.

"Bullshit," Liz replied.

"Right? Well, then Mary cornered me later after Alannah went to her about me, apparently, and told me that Alannah is actually severely anorexic, and her Mormon family sent her here for the marijuana she used to ease her pain from starving herself. So, Alannah hates me now. Which is fun."

"Shut . . . up," she whisper-yelled.

"Swear," I said, nodding. "We can talk about it later," I added, pointing to the person leading the meeting.

I would be lying if I said I wasn't disappointed that Alannah wasn't getting high. Don't get me wrong: I wouldn't wish addiction on my worst enemy; it's just that a small part of me was really hoping to score some drugs from her, and now that option was out the window. So if getting high wasn't on the table, I guess I'd just have to try to shift my focus to recovery.

It started with this meeting.

Devon, the chairman, couldn't have been older than seventeen. I couldn't help but feel a bit sad that he'd already managed to find himself *here* by his age.

"At this time the meeting is open. Would anyone like to share? Yes, Marco," Devon said, pointing to a man with a face tattoo wearing a giant gold chain I could see all the way across the room.

"I'm Marco, I'm an addict," he began.

"Hi, Marco!" everyone chorused in greeting.

"I've been struggling lately, you know. I know I'm not supposed to use drugs, and I know I'm supposed to stick with people in recovery, but it's hard. Life is boring as shit now. I'm just working, collecting a paycheck, and going home to sit in my apartment. All I can think about is how much fun I used to have banging dope and stealing cars . . . Shit was exciting. Like, once, my boy Paco and I jacked this Suburban and scrapped it for parts. We got like two grand and spent the night partying. Like, that's the shit that gets my heart pumping, you know?"

He seemed too excited reminiscing about this, so I tuned him out. What he was saying wasn't helpful to me; in fact, it made me want to get high. But I agreed with everything he described. Life in recovery was in fact stressful and boring as shit.

Marco eventually wrapped it up and everyone thanked him. The next person raised their hand and began to share.

"Hi, everyone, I'm Willa and I'm an addict. What was just shared really resonated with me. I vividly recall having those same thoughts and feelings when I first got clean . . ."

The woman speaking had short blond hair and was wearing a headband with flowers on it, like real flowers. She was beautiful and gave off an earth-mother vibe. "Filling that huge void left behind by my drug of choice was difficult at first. I didn't know what to put there. But over time—and with the help of everyone here—I was able to slowly but surely fill up that space with things that brought me joy. The more time I spent working on myself and with others in recovery, the easier it got. So, to anyone who feels bored or lost, give it time: Your blessings are coming."

Damn, I needed to hear that.

"I am so grateful to be here with all of you today because normally today is a tough day for me," she continued. "It's the anniversary of my mother's death." My eyebrows raised, and I listened intently. "My mother died of cancer very suddenly, and unfortunately I was in active addiction and wasn't able to be present for her at the time, so this day is always hard."

This was one of those moments in meetings that gave me chills. I went through the same exact thing with my mother. As she continued speaking, I listened in awe. It was like she was telling *my* story.

"Thank you, Willa," everyone said in unison as she finished.

In the recovery community, a sponsor is someone with a year

or more clean, who's been through all twelve steps of the program. My last sponsor was currently in the midst of a meth binge, so I had to find someone new. As someone who hated rejection, the idea of asking a stranger to help me made me want to die. It probably stemmed from the time I passed Justin Carver a note in middle school asking him to be my boyfriend, then watching in horror as he made a disgusted face and passed it to his friends. I heard he ended up becoming a door-to-door vacuum salesman, and the idea of him being rejected countless times a day brought me joy.

I knew by the way my heart was racing that I was going to ask Willa to be my sponsor. Not only would it check one thing off my list, but she seemed like she had some wisdom to share. Plus, we had the whole dead mom thing in common.

As the meeting ended, I took a deep breath, mustered up all the courage I could, and headed toward where Willa was standing. "Hi, Willa. I'm Tiffany," I said, boldly entering the girly circle she was standing in. "I really loved what you shared, and was wondering if you'd be willing to sponsor me . . ." I blurted.

She turned all the way around to face me and paused for what seemed like an eternity, before smiling and responding . . .

"No."

14

—

WHAT LITTLE PRIDE I HAD LEFT DISAPPEARED LIKE A CLOUD of smoke. "Yikes . . . Ah . . . this is awkward," I said. I mean, good for her for having strong boundaries, but *damn*. Her laid-back hippie vibe had hidden what a hard-ass she was. "I'm sorry, but I've never asked someone before . . . to sponsor me. I should have probably spoken to you a bit more first, I just . . . sorry to bother you." I nodded and swiveled on my heels so I could run away as quickly as possible.

She spoke suddenly. "I should clarify . . ."

I swiveled back around. "No, I mean, you were pretty clear. Very clear. Like, alarmingly clear . . ."

"I'm sorry, my personality doesn't go over well with people at first. I'm working on it. But, listen, I'm not saying no as in, not ever . . ."

Well, this is annoying.

"I never commit to sponsoring unless someone commits to

me first." Her tone was almost flat, like she'd had this conversation a thousand times and was bored of it.

"All right, commit . . . how? Do I need to take you on a date? What's up?"

A few girls chuckled, and so did Willa, which was a relief. "No, silly. I just mean, I'm happy to sponsor you, but I want to make sure you *really* want recovery first, so you have to work for it. Call me for the next eleven days. One call a day. If I don't answer, just leave a voicemail telling me about your day. If you do that, I'll agree to sponsor you."

Part of me was irritated with the way she dangled her sponsorship in front of me like a carrot. Did she think she was better than me? The other, perhaps larger part of me realized that in all honesty, she probably *was* better than me. She had put in her time and done the work required to stay clean. She had navigated life in recovery and learned lessons along the way. She had something I didn't have, which was wisdom from experience.

I needed it. I needed her to help me, so I had to humble myself.

I thrust my hand forward. "You got a deal." I shook her hand once she placed it in mine. Sealing the deal that I would do whatever it took to have her sponsor me. I regretted it almost immediately. Knowing me, I'd surely fuck it up in no time.

It had been ten days since I'd met Willa, and I'd managed to call every day. I'd been searching for a job to no avail and trying to repair relationships with my family while simultaneously learning to make it through each day without drugs. It wasn't easy, and frankly, I was getting bored.

"Hey, it's Willa. Leave me a message and I'll call you back!"
Beep.

I had already left multiple awkward, rambling voicemails for the woman I wanted to be my sponsor and now it was time to make another strange deposit in her inbox. "Heyyyy, Willa. It's Tiffany. Again. Just calling to uh, check in, I guess. It's been a pretty eventful day. I hung out with my roommates, then went out to look for a job. Um . . . Just left a meeting . . . So . . . that's about it."

I paused, debating whether or not to hang up.

"Actually, that's not it," I said, pacing the sidewalk. "So, I gotta be honest with you. I'm bored as shit. I'm not used to being bored. I'm used to chaos and fast-paced, sketchy illegal shit. I mean, don't get me wrong, it's nice not being a slave to the drug, it's just . . . Is this it? Like, is this what life is like in recovery? Also, I feel like something bad is going to happen for some reason, and it's scaring me. I can't put my finger on it, but it's like a looming sense of dread. I don't know, I'm rambling. I still haven't found a job and rent is due soon. That's scaring me too. I guess my main emotion, at the moment, is fear. But that's the thing, my emotions are like a jack-in-the-box. I never know which one is gonna pop up. And I don't have the right tools to, like, deal with them. So I'm really looking forward to tomorrow because it's day eleven and I could really use some guidance. Anyway, I just needed to get that off my chest. Also—"

"To send your message now, press one or hang up, to listen to your message, press seven. To erase and re-record, press nine."

Jesus, even the voicemail lady is sick of my shit.

My finger hovered over the nine button.

Screw it. I hit the number one button and hung up.

I arrived home and practically fell through the front door with exhaustion. I'd spent the day handing in applications, same as yesterday and the day before. Another day of coming home empty-handed was taking a toll on me. I needed sleep. Lots of it.

I trudged to the bedroom door and pulled it open. It took a moment for my eyes to adjust to the darkness, but when they did my hands flew to my chest and I froze in place. "What the fuck?" I turned to leave and find someone, and I slammed into Sam, who was standing directly behind me.

"Sorry! I heard you come in," she said, grabbing my shoulders to steady me.

"It's fine, um . . . Where the hell is all of Liz's stuff? Her bed is stripped and her drawers are open and they're empty," I asked, pointing behind me. "Did she switch rooms?"

"She's gone," Sam said, shaking her head.

"What?!" I snapped. "What do you mean? She died?" I asked, feeling my knees start to give out.

"What? No, no. She's alive. More alive than she's been in a while," she laughed, pulling up her sagging pants.

"What does that even mean?"

"She got high, Tiffany. Mary kicked her out. She's gone."

15

—

"WHAT?!" I EXCLAIMED. MY EYEBROWS LIFTED SO HIGH THEY
were practically in my hairline.

"Yeah, she was in there," she said, pointing to the bathroom.
"I guess she stood up too quickly and slammed her head into the
bathroom wall. Mary heard it and came running. There were
needles, pills, all that shit."

I frantically patted down my pockets until I located my phone.
With a shaky hand I unlocked the screen and called Liz's phone.
It rang once and went straight to voicemail.

"It's dead," Sam said. "I already tried."

"What . . . the fuck," I snapped, calling it again.

"At least you added a couple other words to 'What?!' that
time," she said, laughing.

I narrowed my eyes at her. "This isn't funny. We need to find
her and get her help!"

"Help? Girl . . . you're crazy. She don't want help. She wants to get high. I don't think it's funny either, Miss Ma'am, but once you hang around people in recovery long enough, you get comfortable with the harsh truth that sometimes you gotta step over some dead bodies on your journey."

"What?! That's horrible. How can you even say that? She's not even dead, so that doesn't make sense." I shook my head and tried Liz's phone again.

"It's an expression. Obviously, you aren't stepping over, like, dead bodies, but lots of people you love are gonna fall off the cliff. You gotta learn to keep going, cuz you aren't in a place to save anybody—you can't even save yourself. So if you stop and try to pick that body up and save it, it's gonna slow you down, and your addiction is gonna catch up and take you out with them."

I exhaled sharply. What she was saying made sense, but I couldn't just "let her go" and keep walking. I *could* help Liz. It wasn't too late. I could help her get into treatment, or remind her that her life was worth living . . . I could convince her to get clean. I could.

"I see your mind racing," Sam said, crossing her arms and leaning against the wall. "You don't have to do nothing. You can pray for her . . . and call your sponsor."

I rolled my eyes and swallowed down my frustration. "Whatever," I mumbled, walking into my room and slamming the door.

The next morning, I picked up my phone and dialed Willa's number. When the voice said "Hello!" I was preparing to leave a message.

"Oh my gosh, you answered," I said, sitting straight up in bed.

"Of course I did! It's day eleven. I'm so proud of you, Tiff—can I call you Tiff? I feel like I know you now from listening to your voicemails."

I dug my nails into the palm of my hand and laughed nervously. To say I was embarrassed would be an understatement.

"Yes, you can call me Tiff. Sorry about the voicemails, I wasn't sure what to say. This feels super awkward."

"You did great. Most people don't make it to day eleven, so . . . yay. Anyway, what are you up to?"

"Well, I'm sitting on my bed because my roommate relapsed and . . ."

"Oh no," she said sympathetically.

"Yeah . . . I'm kind of struggling with it, so, anyway, I'm going crazy."

"Send me your address."

"Do what now?"

"Send me your address. I'm coming to pick you up."

I hesitated. "Oh. Um . . . What are we going to . . . Why are you going to pick me up?"

"We are gonna hit a meeting," she said simply.

"Actually, I already have a meeting planned for tonight—my cousin is graduating from rehab so I'm gonna go there. It's like a meeting-slash-commencement. My sister will be there, and I haven't seen her in a while. I'm hoping today will show her how much I've changed. So . . . can't really miss this meeting!"

"Cool . . . you can do both. Send me your address," she repeated.

My cheeks flushed with anger. "I really need to look for a job . . ." I protested.

"You really don't know what you need. That's part of the problem."

This. Bitch.

"Listen, I know what it's like to feel 'behind' in life. It feels like you should spend every spare moment trying to catch up. I get it. But there's a difference between being busy and being productive—and going to a meeting when you're struggling is the definition of productive. Yes, a job is important, but your recovery is more important. You will lose anything you put before your recovery, so let's go to a meeting, then after that you can look for a job until you're blue in the face."

I wanted to hang up the phone and throw it. I have an issue with authority, and it felt like she was bossing me around, but I suddenly remembered something my first sponsor told me and it gave me pause. She'd said, "If anyone in recovery invites you to do something recovery-related, say yes and commit before your brain talks you out of it."

I gave her NuStep's address.

"Heading that way. I'll see you soon." *Click.*

After the meeting, Willa drove me back to the house. Her car smelled like patchouli and she had an amethyst hanging from the rearview mirror. "Protection," she said, staring straight ahead.

"What was that?" I asked.

"The crystal. It's for protection."

I nodded and smiled, but I secretly wondered how it would save her from breaking bones and crushing vital organs during a crash.

After the meeting, I was thankful she'd forced me to go. Being there reminded me that everyone has their own issues and problems in life, but staying clean during those trials is what matters most. I closed my eyes and listened, feeling particularly grateful for the opportunity to be free from jail, enjoying fellowship with another recovering addict.

"Thank you so much for taking me," I said, unbuckling my seatbelt once we'd arrived back at my place.

"I brought you this worksheet—it's step one of the twelve steps." She handed me a stack of papers. "I know you've done it before, but as our lives change, so do our answers. Take some time and fill this out. We can go over the questions next week."

"Awesome! Thank you," I said, pretending to be excited. She was right, I *had* done these steps before, and step one was the most pointless of all. For me, anyway. All the questions are based around admitting we are powerless over drugs and alcohol, and clearly I'd already admitted and accepted that I was an addict. I was living in a halfway house.

"You're welcome. Thank you for coming tonight. Even though I didn't really give you a choice," she laughed, reaching out for a hug. I leaned over and gave her an awkward side hug.

"Yeah, you basically kidnapped me, but you're welcome." I smiled.

"Hey, I want you to keep calling me, okay? This part of your recovery can be the toughest, and I promise there isn't a problem you'll experience that me or another fellow addict haven't experienced. We can help, you just gotta ask."

"I will, I promise. Thanks for the worksheet," I said, holding it up.

"Yup, have fun at your meeting tonight."

Shit, I'd forgotten all about the meeting and my cousin's graduation. I checked my phone and saw that I had more than enough time to take a nap, so instead of rushing out to find a job, I decided to rest.

That was the plan, anyway, until I walked into my bedroom and found a naked woman crouched down near my bed.

16

—

"I KNOW I'VE ALREADY SAID IT, BUT I AM *REALLY* SORRY." I said after leaving then reentering my room.

"No, don't apologize, it's my fault. I should have locked the door . . ." Luckily, this woman—whoever the hell she was—had put some clothes on.

"I honestly wasn't expecting anyone to be in here. I mean, I figured eventually someone would be . . . just not this soon."

"I'm Elyse," the girl said. "I got the call this morning that a bed had become available suddenly. I'd been on a waiting list, so I was really thrilled. I'm surprised they didn't tell you."

Me too.

"Well, cool, I'm glad it worked out for you," I said, suddenly feeling like this room no longer belonged to me. Elyse looked like a bitch. I'm not sure if it was because she reminded me of every mean girl I'd ever seen in a movie about popular kids versus nerds, or if it was the way her sentences went up at the end like she was asking a question. Either way, I could tell right away that we weren't going to click.

"I'm Tiffany, by the way." I forced a smile, trying to hide that I was devastated they'd filled Liz's spot already, especially without giving me a heads-up. "I was gonna take a nap. I hope you don't mind," I said, slipping beneath the covers. I really didn't give a shit whether she minded or not. This was my room first.

"In the middle of the day?" she laughed.

I clenched my jaw. *Yes, bitch, that's when naps take place.* "Yep, I'm exhausted."

"I'm jealous. I have to go to work."

My eyebrows furrowed in confusion. "You have a job already?"

"Uh-huh, my boss let me keep my job while I was in rehab. Perks of having your mom own a restaurant, I guess." She laughed again.

Must be nice. To have a job and a mom.

"I'll leave the room so I don't disturb you," she added, standing up from the bed and grabbing her phone.

"No, it's okay, you don't have to . . ."

"It's fine," she whispered. "I can get ready in the bathroom. Sleep well."

I rolled my eyes and turned to face the wall. I couldn't look at her side; the way her stuff was sitting on Liz's nightstand made my blood boil. I closed my eyes and within minutes was fast asleep.

My dad and sister, Laney, picked me up after my nap, and when we entered the auditorium where my cousin Geo's meeting and graduation were being held, I spotted him up on stage right away. I gave him a quick wave as I took my seat. The ceremony began as usual, with a speech about recovery. As I listened to the words, my eyes drifted up to the stage where the seven people commencing the program were seated. I looked at their smiling faces, each so full of hope and optimism. They looked healthy and happy, surely a marked difference from when they'd first arrived here.

Suddenly my eyes stopped short when they reached the man seated next to Geo. He towered over the rest of the men on stage, and his broad, muscular shoulders rippled beneath his long-sleeve button-down. When he smiled, my heart caught in my chest. His eyes had an intensity to them, and their bright green color next to his jet-black hair was offensively attractive. He was the kind of man you look at once and immediately recognize that every other person in the room was lusting for him right along with you.

A high-pitched squeal from the back of the room startled me from the hypnotizing love spell I'd been under.

"Daddy, Daddy!"

Everyone in the room, including myself, turned to look at what kind of creature was capable of producing such a banshee-like screech. I saw a flash of pink as a toddler wearing a princess dress darted down the aisle toward the stage while a petite blond woman with her arms outstretched chased after her. I smiled, thinking how sweet the little girl looked, and my jaw dropped open as I watched my handsome prince scoop her up and place her on his lap.

The imaginary hearts floating above my head began to pop one by one. Of course he was married and had a child. FUCK my life.

The speech ended and the graduation portion of the program

began. Geo stood up, and my family started hooting and hollering as he walked to the podium to say a few words. We were the loudest ones there and didn't bother trying to hide it. I was so proud of Geo. He'd been through so much and had made it out alive.

My heart started to bounce wildly when I noticed my imaginary ex-boyfriend had stood up to take his turn at the podium. He was just as tall as I'd imagined, maybe taller.

"Hi, I'm Colin . . ." he said shakily, pausing to clear his throat. He seemed nervous. Should I run up and comfort him with a make-out session? *No . . . Shut up, Tiffany.*

"I am grateful to be clean today and have the opportunity to be the father my daughter, Addison, deserves. I look forward to being the son my mother had hoped for, and the brother my sisters need." He paused and took another deep breath before continuing, "I didn't care about life before. In fact, I often thought that the world would be better off without me. I know now that I have purpose, and I've never wanted anything more than I want my sobriety. I have been given a second chance at life, and I promise I am going to make the most of it." His bottom lip started to quiver, and he looked up from his paper and out into the crowd. "Mom, thank you for loving me when I didn't deserve it, and for taking care of my daughter when I couldn't. I promise to fight every day and show you that all the work you put into raising me wasn't for nothing. I want to thank my sister, Sasha, for coming to visit every family day. I couldn't have made it through this experience without you."

I looked to my left just as the blond woman who'd been chasing his daughter earlier put her hands on her heart, then blew him a kiss.

Ahhhh . . . she was his *sister*, not his wife.

As he continued to speak my vision blurred with tears. My heart softened at the sound of his voice, and every single heartbeat after that was for him. I looked over at my sister as he spoke and realized she didn't get it . . . the *magnitude* of what he was saying. She didn't grasp the pain behind his words; it was something only a fellow addict could feel. She couldn't see the gleam of hope in his eyes or hear the beautiful sound of gratitude beneath each sentence.

I did. *I felt every syllable.*

I hung on to every single word until he finished speaking, and then when he did, I let out a loud "Woooo!" Unfortunately, my timing was off, and it came out about two seconds before the clapping started. He glanced in my direction and smiled before taking his paper from the podium and heading back to his seat.

I'm pretty sure I was officially in love.

17

I HADN'T REALLY BEEN INTERESTED IN ANYONE—MALE OR female—since Eliot. Not in a real way, anyway. I couldn't *imagine* being in a relationship ever again. I knew anyone would lose interest the minute they found out what I'd done to my last boyfriend, and even if they *did* manage to stick around, I'd eventually find a way to mess it all up.

I was a dangerous person to love.

Besides, they say you shouldn't get into a relationship within your first year of sobriety because it's hard to focus on yourself when your tongue is down someone else's throat. They also say two sick people don't make a well couple and that you shouldn't get distracted by someone who has nothing to offer you in your new life. So far, I'd been pretty good about keeping to myself and focusing on my recovery. But the way that gorgeous Herculean man spoke directly to my soul made me want to try and break the rules. Even just for one hot night . . .

At the end of the ceremony, I ran up to Geo and hugged him. "I'm so proud of you!" I gushed, squeezing him tight.

"Thank you, I'm proud of myself too. And I'm proud of you, dude! Congrats on what, like ten months?"

"Almost! Next month will be ten months."

I pretended not to notice Colin approaching behind him. "So, what are your plans now?" I asked, sucking in my stomach and twirling my hair.

"I'm probably gonna stay here in the graduate dorm for a bit then find a place to live. Hey, this is my boy Colin," he said, pulling him toward all of us and slapping his chest.

I was jealous. I wanted to slap that chest.

I looked at Colin, then toward my sister, and frowned. Of course . . . of course he was eye-banging my beautiful little sister. Laney was tall with long, thick jet-black hair. She was curvy, tan, and tattooed, and the boys (and girls) always went crazy over her. I wanted to donkey-kick her. She had always been the exotic one, and I was the one with a "good personality." Which was basically a nice way for people to say I was the weird creature hobbling beside her like Quasimodo.

God, I hate being the ugly sibling. This happened every time. I finally find my soulmate, and my sister intercepts with her perfect stupid face and her dumb nice hair.

"We gotta get going, girls," Colin said. "Geo, gimme a buzz, let's go to a meeting together or grab lunch sometime."

"Will do. I love you guys, man. Thanks for coming." He went down the line giving each of us a hug, and I decided to take this opportunity to address Colin.

"Congratulations on graduating tonight." I smiled.

"Thank you very much," he replied with a nod.

"Yeah . . . I'm in recovery too. I've got almost ten months clean. I know how tough it is and the strength it takes to quit."

"Oh wow, congratulations. That's awesome," he said, seemingly uninterested.

"Are you in recovery too?" he asked Laney.

I rolled my eyes.

"Nooooo . . . no, I'm not. I'm just here to support them," she said, gesturing toward us druggies.

"Wow, that's nice of you. Very cool."

Oh, come on . . . I wanted to yell out that she was a bartender at a strip club and that it would never work out between them because she loved weed, but I decided against it.

"All right, you guys, I'll catch you later," he said, waving.

"Bye, Geo!" I called after him. "NICE MEETING YOU, Colin!" I screamed, a bit too aggressively. He turned back, looking confused, and gave a nervous wave.

"He was cute," Laney said as we walked back to the car.

I wanted to karate-chop her neck.

On the ride back to the halfway house, we joked like old times. Dad did his famous Robin Williams impression while Laney and I laughed so hard we cried. It felt good to be with them. It felt like home.

We were having so much fun that I'd all but forgotten about Colin.

Which is why it came as such a shock later that night when I received a message request on Facebook from him.

18

HEY, THANK YOU FOR COMING TO MY COMMENCEMENT TO-
night, that was really sweet of you.

My heart skipped a beat, but I tried to play it cool.

*Well, technically I was there for my cousin, but you're wel-
come, glad I could support you.* I reread it six times before tapping Send.

As soon as the message was delivered, a feeling of dread replaced the butterflies inside my stomach.

Holy shit, he thinks I'm my sister.

*I was just joking. I know you were there to see Geo, he's my
boy. Hey listen, so I just got my phone back tonight and the very
first thing I wanted to do was tell you how beautiful I thought you
were.*

Great. It was confirmed. He thought I was Laney. I threw myself back onto the pillow and sighed, trying to figure out the least
embarrassing way to break the news to him.

Yikes. Well, this is awkward. I think you have the wrong sister, lol, I'm Tiffany. Laney is my sister, the one with the long hair. Haha.

I wrote "Haha" so he would know I was cool with his mistake and not seconds away from crying into my pillow.

I logged off Facebook and went to the kitchen for a snack, but before I could reach the cabinet, a ping from my phone sent me running full-speed back to the room.

I know exactly who you are, dork. You're Tiffany. Geo told me all about you after you guys left. He actually had a lot of amazing things to say about you. He also said he thought you might have been flirty with me, something about the way you were staring. Anyway, I always thought you were a lesbian. But then he told me about your ex-boyfriend.

My jaw fell open and my eyes went round.

What?! What did he say about my ex? Why did you think I was a lesbian? I have so many questions, LOL.

Three little dots appeared at the bottom of our message exchange, and my heart thumped as I stared at them, like they were lottery numbers.

Well, I saw you making out with a girl in that van outside a meeting once when I came out to smoke. Geo just said your ex had you arrested for theft or something.

He saw me making out with someone? Oh . . . Yeah. I did do that. It's a long story and a confusing time in my life. I don't even remember her name—she got re-arrested from rehab for lighting a fire at a bank or something.

Yeah, I can see how that would have given off lesbian vibes. Anyway, I'm bisexual. But that's neither here nor there . . . So you're reaching out to me just to tell me I'm beautiful?

Yes. Among other things. As you know, I just commenced the program, so I'm trying to get connected with other people in recovery.

That's a good idea, I believe you're supposed to reach out to other men though, lol.

Whoops. I'll definitely do that. While I have you though, would you like to go out to dinner sometime?

The butterflies came back in full force. A smile slowly spread across my face as I imagined him picking me up and taking me out. He was *so* handsome. Suddenly my smile faded when the rational part of my brain kicked in. This guy just graduated from rehab. The fact that his first instinct was to start messaging girls instead of focusing on himself was a red flag. And I was in no position to date either.

Listen, you are . . . really attractive, and you seem nice. But I just got out of a terrible situation and really need to focus on my recovery. To say I'm flattered would be an understatement, and I assure you . . . there's nothing I'd love more than to go on a date with you. I just know it isn't a good idea.

The three dots appeared at the bottom, and I could hardly breathe. What the hell was I doing? This was the most attractive man that had ever shown interest in me, and I was rejecting him. I felt like an idiot.

I completely understand and respect your decision. It actually makes me like you more, somehow. Let's not go on a date then. We can just be friends and get to know each other. Would that be okay?

I shook my head, knowing there was no way he was going to stick around if I wasn't putting out. The guy had been locked up in rehab for four months. If I wasn't going to give him any, it wouldn't take long for him to find it elsewhere.

Yes, that sounds good. Friends it is.

I knew right away . . . that he and I were *not* going to just be friends.

19

—

"FANCY MEETING YOU HERE," COLIN SAID, HOLDING OUT HIS arms for a hug as he approached me. After nonstop texting for a week—plus a few calls—we'd decided to meet each other in person. What made it easier was that he'd moved into a halfway house within walking distance of mine.

"Yeah, this is so weird. You know, I usually don't hug random men I find walking down the street, but you're pretty cute." I wrapped my arms around his waist. His abs were rock hard.

"You smell nice," I mumbled into his chest as we hugged. *"You smell nice"? What the hell, Tiffany.*

"Thanks, you do too."

"I showered," I said, regretting it immediately.

He laughed. "Well, that's good."

I cringed and tried not to obsess about how awkward I always had to make things.

"Wow, you are even more beautiful than I remember," he said

suddenly, looking me up and down. My stomach did a somersault.

"Thank you," I squeaked, running my fingers through my hair nervously.

"Are you ready to go in?" he asked, holding out his hand for me to grab. I looked down at it.

"Friends don't hold hands, remember?" I teased, before slipping my hand into his. Somehow joking about being "just friends" made me feel protected. But I could physically feel myself slipping down that slope, and instead of making a true effort to stop myself, I allowed myself to continue sliding down. Down into the unknown. Down into a place where most of my thoughts consisted of him. I knew it was wrong, but I couldn't help it.

As we waited to be seated, I stole a few quick glances in his direction. I couldn't fathom how somebody this attractive would want to hang out with me. Maybe it stemmed from childhood, when I was always picked on for my looks and was invisible to the opposite sex. I was always the "funny" friend who guys went to for dating advice and to "put a good word in" for them. So having a guy that looked like Colin be interested in me . . . It seemed too good to be true.

"Any luck finding a job?" he asked as soon as we were seated and food had arrived.

I rolled my eyes. "None, dude. It's so stupid. Luckily Mary is being nice about the late rent, but I have to pay it by Friday or she's gonna kick me out." I took a long sip of my Oreo milkshake and immediately regretted it. "Oh my God!" I yelled, opening my mouth and shoving my thumb inside.

"What is happening right now?" he laughed, quickly looking around.

"I have a brain freeth," I mumbled.

"A what?"

I removed my thumb out of my mouth. "A brain freeze. I think I'm dying," I said, putting it back in.

He laughed and wiped his face with a napkin. "Is there anything I can do? You want me to call an ambulance?"

I held up my middle finger and laughed. He was adorable and funny, and I wanted to have his children.

"What was that thing you did, with your thumb?"

"Oh . . . it's something my dad taught me. Apparently if you push your thumb up into the roof of your mouth it warms your brain up quicker or something. I don't know why, but it helps."

"I really like you," he blurted, his expression suddenly serious.

"What?" I asked, taken aback.

"I do. I know we are just friends, but I can't help it. I like you. I think you're hilarious, and you're so strong in your recovery. I just . . . I don't know. I'm just feeling really optimistic about this whole 'life without drugs' thing, and I think being around you is good for me."

My heart sank. There it was. That's why he was interested in me. I knew he meant it to be a compliment, but I was able to read between the lines. He wasn't so much interested in me—as a person—I was just the first girl in recovery he'd met, and he thought I could be a good influence for him.

"Listen," I said, gently placing my napkin on the table and exhaling, "if you think I'm going to be good for your recovery, or somehow be able to keep you on track or fix you or something, you're wrong . . ."

"No, that's not what I . . ."

"It's the opposite, actually. The first few months of recovery are crucial, and you should just be focusing on yourself, and surrounding yourself with strong men who can help you. I am not the person you want to look to for guidance or to be a positive influence. I can't even take care of myself. I have nothing to offer, so if you were hoping . . ."

"Tiffany . . . stop."

I stopped talking, even though there was so much more I wanted to say.

"Why are you doing that?" he asked, his eyes softer, almost pleading.

"Doing what?" I shrugged. "I'm not doing anything, I just . . . You said you think being around me is good for you, and I am here to tell you that it's not. I'm just being honest. Anyone who gets close to me ends up getting hurt, and I don't want that to happen to you."

He slowly shook his head, and I realized this meal would be our first and last together.

"Why are you doing that?" he repeated. "You're shutting down and trying to push me away." He looked like he was trying to hide his smile, like he somehow found this amusing.

"I'm not doing either of those things," I said, crossing my arms.

"You're doing both of those things actually." He smirked, the gleam in his eye making my legs tingle. "I do the same thing, that's why I can spot it," he said, popping a fry into his mouth. "When things start going good, it feels too good to be true. I usually end up sabotaging things before they have a chance to sabotage me. That's what you're doing," he said, pointing a fry at me, "and you need to stop." He smiled.

I shook my head and laughed.

He continued: "I think you're right, we do need to focus on ourselves first. But I don't see any harm in hanging out and having fun. I'm not expecting you to marry me or anything, I'm just saying . . . I like you. And you're worthy of being liked. So please just . . . stop trying to find reasons this won't work out, and let's just see what happens."

I nodded and felt myself let go of the imaginary shield I was holding up between us.

"Dinner was fun, thank you so much," I said about an hour later, opening my arms for a hug at the end of my driveway. Instead of reciprocating the hug, he scratched his head nervously and took a step back.

"Oh, I'm sorry . . . We don't have to hug. I just . . . Yikes. This is awkward." I laughed, wanting to run out in front of the car that was passing us. The headlights lit up his face momentarily, and I noticed it was shiny, like he was sweating or something.

"Can I kiss you?" he asked suddenly, stopping my heart in its tracks.

"Oh." I dropped my arms to my side, completely dumbfounded.

"I haven't stopped thinking about kissing you since we first sat down at the restaurant," he said, taking a step closer. I placed my hand on my stomach, trying to slow down the violent fluttering of the butterflies there.

"It's okay if you don't want to . . ." he began.

"I do!" I shouted. "Want to . . . I mean."

My heart thumped wildly. I wasn't mentally prepared for this.

"Are you sure?" he asked, taking another step toward me and gently sliding his hand behind my neck.

My knees felt weak, and I couldn't speak. I nodded eagerly

and closed my eyes until I felt his warm lips on mine. My heart was racing so quickly that I thought I might faint. He gripped me tight and I melted into him, digging my nails into the back of his neck. He smiled briefly, then devoured my lips once again.

"It's almost curfew," he whispered.

"Yeah . . ." I replied, reluctantly pulling away from him.

"We'll have to do this again sometime." His appreciative gaze traveled down my body. I nodded, feeling so giddy I thought I might float away. I hadn't felt this way in as long as I could remember. "I'll text you in the morning," he added, leaning down and planting another peck on my lips.

"Okay, yes. Good night." I smiled and waved him off. Then I watched him walk away until he was out of sight and let out a squeal. I couldn't believe we'd just kissed. I couldn't believe we'd gone on a date.

I inhaled deeply and swiveled on my heels to head up the driveway, and that was when I saw her.

It was Mary, standing in the garage with her arms crossed, glaring at me like she'd just witnessed a murder.

Shit . . . This was not going to be good.

20

"WHAT WAS THAT?" MARY ASKED, CLASPING HER HANDS TO-gether on top of the table where we were sitting.

"What was what?"

"Who was the man you were making out with at the end of my driveway?"

I knew we weren't supposed to fraternize—this was clearly stated in the house rules—but to be honest I was hoping it was more of a suggestion. I mean, how could they ban us from dating? I didn't think that was legal or natural.

"It was . . . a man . . ." I began.

"Yes, I already said that," she replied.

I nodded. "Right. So, it was a man . . . named Colin."

"Okay, and how do you know Colin?" she demanded.

"Well . . . he's a friend of my cousin's . . ." I was speaking slowly and staring down at her hands. Avoiding eye contact seemed much easier than looking into her beady little eyes.

She craned her neck forward, shaking her head and raising her eyebrows, a cue for me to keep talking.

"He . . . is a man . . . that I met . . ."

"Jesus Christ . . . Are you having a medical episode or something?" she interrupted. "Why are you talking like someone with a concussion right now?" She pushed her glasses higher on the bridge of her nose to get a better look at me.

"Okay. I'm sorry. I just—" I took a deep breath. Clearly I wasn't going to be able to talk myself out of trouble. Breaking the rules was grounds for dismissal from the house, and given that I still didn't have a job to pay rent, it would be an easy decision for her to make. "I met him at my cousin's graduation a few weeks back. Tonight was the first night we hung out, I swear. We've been talking on the phone, and I honestly didn't think it was going to go anywhere. I didn't even think I liked men anymore . . ." Well, that wasn't exactly true, but I was grasping for proof of my innocence.

She raised an eyebrow and I realized I probably could have left that last part out.

"Anyway, he was just somebody outside of the house I could talk to. We really are just friends . . . We were supposed to be, anyway. I told him I wasn't ready to date. That kiss . . . was just as surprising to me as it was to you."

Her face switched from anger to concern. "Did he force himself on you?" She leaned forward in her chair to get closer. Her anger seemed to have subsided, and for a split second I contemplated lying to prevent myself from getting in trouble.

Out of nowhere, Willa's stupid voice popped into my head. It was something she'd said to me on the way home from the meeting. "If you're having trouble making a decision, or don't know what the right thing to do in a situation is, the best way to handle it is by doing the opposite of what the old you would have done. If the old you would have stepped over a piece of paper on the floor, the new you should bend down, pick it up, and throw it in the trash. Most of the decisions we made in active addiction were terrible, so chances are—at least until we spend enough time in recovery—whatever it is we *want* to do . . . we should probably do the opposite."

"No," I blurted. "No, he didn't force himself on me at all. He actually asked permission. To which I said yes. I had plenty of time and opportunity to say no. I just didn't want to."

"Okay then." She leaned back in her chair and nodded, her lips turned downward in disapproving surprise.

"I know it was wrong," I pleaded. "I do. It's just . . . ever since I left rehab I've felt like a failure. All day, every day. I can't get a job to save my life, I have no money . . . my sleep schedule is off, and I spend most of the night staring at my ceiling replaying all the things I've done and people I've hurt. I have no friends, and the one friend I did have is gone, off walking the streets and using. I can't . . . I'm really struggling to find the point in getting clean. I mean, it's nice not to wake up every day feeling like shit physically . . . but I still wake up feeling like shit . . . just . . . emotionally. The guilt and shame is so heavy and the fact that no one wants to hire me because I'm a felon just further solidifies my belief that I will never be good enough. Now that I'm an addict with a record, no matter how hard I try . . . that's all I'll ever be."

Tears of frustration formed in my eyes and before Mary could respond, I continued.

"Anyway, I don't know who I am anymore, and when I met Colin . . . I don't know, for the first time in a long time I felt worthy. He made me laugh and forget about how tragic my life has become. He distracted me from the reality that no one will ever trust or respect me again, and it felt really good, and . . ."

She put her hand up to stop me, and I exhaled loudly.

"I want to stop you right there," she said softly, reaching across the table to grab my hand. I wanted to snatch it away. I hate being touched when I'm emotional.

"I want you to know that everything you just said is valid. I hear you, and I see you." She was squeezing my hand and looking deep into my eyes. "I believe you feel that way, I really do. But the harsh reality is . . . you're wrong."

I opened my mouth to defend myself, and she let go of me and held up her hand to stop me again. "Listen . . . listen to me. Recovery is hard, getting acclimated to the world after seeing it through a foggy lens for so long is hard. I get it. I was there once too, and things weren't happening fast enough for me, and I wanted to throw in the towel . . ."

"It's not that things aren't happening fast enough for me, it's just . . ."

"Buuuut . . ." she interrupted. "But you just said it yourself. You've proved my point about why these rules exist and you didn't even realize it." She must have read the annoyance on my face. "You just told me that this guy was distracting you from reality."

"That's not . . . how I meant it."

"In your own words, you said he makes you forget about your life by distracting you. You are using him to fill a void within you, the same way you used to use drugs to forget. To distract you from the reality of being an addict. This is no different, apart from the fact that he is a human being with feelings and emotions, who—by the way—also happens to be in early recovery. I know it feels good, Tiffany." She leaned closer and grabbed my hand again. "I really do, but you are only postponing your misery. You have a lot of work to do on yourself, and it starts with actually doing the work. The answers to life aren't going to fall into your lap, and they certainly won't arrive in the form of a hunky guy. Life out here is hard, but the only way to get through it is to go through it. To experience it, to *feel* it."

I sank back into my chair as realization dawned. I had gotten angry at Colin earlier when I thought he was "using" me for his recovery. In actuality, I was using him. The adrenaline rush of having someone so gorgeous fawning over me gave me the same feelings drugs used to.

"You're right," I murmured.

"I have been doing this for a long time, and it's one of the main reasons people in early recovery end up relapsing. They lose sight of themselves and their goals and devote all their energy to another person. Two sick people don't make a well couple."

I closed my eyes and rolled them. I'd heard that so many friggin' times it made me wanna puke.

"You're right, I'll stop talking to him," I said with a newfound determination. "I have to."

"You do, and you'll see . . . Once you start loving yourself, your partner will be a wonderful addition to your journey. I am proud of you, Tiffany. For doing the right thing. You're stronger than you think." She gave my arm one last squeeze.

"Thank you for talking to me about this, I really needed to hear it. I am ready to focus on myself and do what needs to be done to succeed in recovery—whatever it takes."

She gave a proud nod and smiled before heading to her bedroom. I waited until I heard her door click shut, to ensure she wasn't going to turn for a last-minute eviction. I couldn't believe she was letting me stay despite breaking the rules.

I knew she was right about Colin. It would definitely be in my best interest to break things off before they got serious. I needed to dedicate my life to recovery and the steps and my higher power, not some guy with a kid who was probably going to end up breaking my heart anyway.

An hour later, I stared at the long text I'd crafted for Colin, in which I kindly and clearly stated that although I was head-over-heels crazy for him, I could no longer pursue a relationship with him. I let him know that while he consumed my every thought and took my breath away regularly, that we couldn't be together because we hadn't been clean long enough and would likely derail our efforts to recover from addiction.

My finger hovered over the Send button for what seemed like an eternity. One click and my only source of happiness these days would be gone forever. As difficult as it would be, it was the right thing to do. I had to send it. I needed to.

Instead, I deleted it and replaced it with "Good night, Sexy."

21

"THIS JOB REQUIRES TONS OF STRENGTH. NO OFFENSE, BUT you're kind of tiny."

I'd just approached a handyman named Tommy at a meeting and had begun begging him for a job.

"Whoa, first of all . . . thank you for calling me tiny. Second of all, I may not be as strong as a full-grown man, but I can assure you I'm more determined and willing than any other prospects. I need a job to keep my bed at the place I'm living, and no one will hire me. I'm desperate."

He seemed to think it over for a moment, then shook his head. "I'm sorry, it's not the right fit." He gave me a quick nod and started to walk away.

"I'll work for free!" I yelled, then winced once the words were out of my mouth.

He turned slowly, looking annoyed, disgusted, and confused. "What?"

"I'm saying . . . I'll work for free for a week so you can see how I work, and then you can hire me. But just a week, because I really need rent."

This felt very drug-addict-y of me, but I was running out of options, and working for someone in recovery was exactly what I needed.

He eyed me up and down, deciding whether I was crazy or not, and shook his head. "Fuck it," he blurted. "Take my card and text me your number. I'll call you tomorrow." He took one last confused look at me and walked away.

A month later, Tommy and I were thick as thieves. He'd been picking me up every morning and I'd proved to him that I was willing to work as hard as any man he could have hired. I was painting houses, putting up drywall, replacing shingles—you name it, I could do it.

Sometimes after work I'd ask Tommy to drop me off at the store near the house. I'd walk to the park behind the neighborhood, where Colin would be waiting with open arms. He and I had managed to keep our relationship under wraps for about a month so far. I replaced his name in my phone as my sister's, and Mary was so pleased to see how much the two of us were communicating.

"See! I told you, it takes time, but familial relationships *can* be repaired," she'd say proudly.

I know it was foolish of me to continue pursuing Colin after what Mary said when she'd caught us kissing, but having to give him up didn't seem fair. Why should I end something wonderful, just because it could *potentially* end badly? What if Colin was my true soulmate and I pushed him away simply because some old people in recovery told me to? It was like instead of pills running through my veins it was hormones, and I couldn't seem to control them.

Willa and I had become close over the past month, and I was truly grateful for that. She knew about Colin, and that was only because she threatened to fire me as her sponsee if I ever lied to her, so I told her almost immediately. Willa also disapproved of my sneaky love affair and would occasionally make remarks like "Maybe you would have finished your stepwork if you hadn't been so busy dry-humping your boyfriend." She blamed all my blunders on Colin, but I didn't mind. I actually found it kind of funny.

My new roommate, Elyse—who I'd finally given a chance—was the only other person I'd confided in about Colin. I knew she wouldn't rat me out because not only had we become best friends, but she too was having a sneaky affair. She was lucky, though. Her boyfriend wasn't an addict and had his own place.

I remember the day I told her that Colin and I had been sneaking off to see each other. I pulled up a photo from his Facebook page and showed her.

Her eyes went round. "Holy shit." She grabbed the phone from me to inspect further. "Oh, I know Colin! We were in rehab together. All the girls were obsessed with hi—" She stopped midsentence once she saw the look of jealousy on my face. "I mean . . . no one liked him. He's a stupid ugly boy."

I laughed and narrowed my eyes at her. "Nice backtrack," I said, shaking my head.

"No, but seriously, Tiff, good for you. He's hot."

"Right? Too hot, actually. Like, I feel like there has to be something wrong with him."

"Maybe he has a small dick. Have you guys had sex?"

"Chilllllll . . ." I said, snatching my phone back. "And no, we haven't. But I did catch a glimpse of it through his pants once when he stood up at a meeting, and girl . . . it is not small."

"So he's hot *and* he's packing? What the hell are you waiting for?"

"Uh, we just met like a month and a half ago. What do you think, I'm some kind of whore?" I laughed.

"Um, didn't you once shave your crotch in a public bathroom so you could hook up with your drug dealer for pills?"

"Whoa. Okay, let's . . . not bring up old stuff, butthole. That was the old me. I'm a new person, thank you very much. Besides, I don't want our first time having intercourse to be behind a dumpster somewhere, and since we both live in halfway houses, that's kind of the only option at this point."

"True, true. Well, unless you get an overnight pass." She smirked.

My eyes suddenly lit up. "Wait, how do I get an overnight pass?"

"How do you not know this? As long as you've been here for a month and your rent is caught up, you can put in a request for a pass. You can spend the night somewhere other than here."

My heart raced with excitement and anticipation. It had never occurred to me to get an overnight pass, because where the hell would I go? Most of my friends resided at sober living, and a sleepover with my sister or dad seemed dangerous. I still didn't quite trust myself around them yet. There was so much history of drinking and smoking weed that just walking into their homes would probably be a trigger.

A hotel, however, was a genius idea. If Colin could get away from his house for the night, we could get a room and spend the entire evening together. No roommates, no rules, just us.

I was basically vibrating with excitement as I knocked on Mary's door to ask for the pass. I didn't even bother asking Colin first—I know he'd be more than willing to spend the night with me. I was going to ask her if I could stay with my sister. Which I knew was a lie, okay. But if I asked permission to spend the night in a hotel so I could repeatedly bang the guy she had told me never to talk to, it probably wouldn't go over well.

She swung open the door and smiled. "Hey there!"

I flashed the sweetest smile I could muster. "Hey, Mary! Do you have a minute? I have a quick question."

"She said yes?" Elyse asked, gripping her coffee mug with both hands and gently blowing the top.

"Yes, dude. I'm freaking out. She told me she'd have to think about it and finally gave me the green light this morning. We are gonna try to do it tomorrow."

I took a bite of my bagel and replayed my conversation with Colin in my head. He sounded so happy when I asked, and when his house manager said he could, he sent me a selfie of his excited face. Followed by a string of dirty texts describing in detail all the things he wanted to do to me. I hadn't been with anyone in so long. The mere thought of getting a whole night with him made my inner thighs tingle.

"If you do go, you have to be careful. I'd be really sad if you got caught and kicked out," she said, spreading cream cheese onto her bagel.

"Awww . . ." I placed a hand over my heart. "That's the nicest thing you've ever said to me," I said with mock admiration.

"Shut up. I'm just saying, it's nice to have someone I can talk to," she muttered, chewing her bagel.

"I know exactly what you mean," I replied. "It takes a while, you know . . . for me to open up to people or whatever. I'm grateful that I ended up with such a cool roommate."

"Okay, let's tone down the mushiness. It's getting weird."

"Agreed," I replied quickly.

"Wait, have you even talked to your sister?" she said suddenly. "Like, what if Mary calls to confirm that's where you're going or whatever?"

That was a good point. I hadn't even thought about it. I wasn't about to call my sister and ask her to lie for me. I used to do that all the time when I was getting high. If I did it now, she'd probably be suspicious and call my dad, freaking out.

Dread suddenly twisted in my gut. If Mary called my sister I'd be screwed . . . and not in the good way.

22

—

I COULDN'T SLEEP. THERE WERE TOO MANY EMOTIONS RUN-
ning rampant inside me: joy about getting an overnight pass, fear
that I might get caught if Mary called my sister, and guilt about
not being forthcoming with my dad and sister about my relationship with Colin.

I didn't know where to put all these emotions, and I didn't like
that. The old me would use a needle and a spoon to shove them
into a box in the back of my mind, but the new me . . . was expected to *feel* them?

Luckily, I was escaping this drama for the night and could forget about the world for a bit. I was finally getting to be alone with
my gorgeous boyfriend, and he would certainly help take my
mind off everything.

"This is crazy." Colin threw his bag on the floor and swooped me
up into his arms. I squealed and giggled and pressed my lips into

his. He gently set me down onto the bed without removing his lips from mine and slowly crawled forward until his body was covering me.

The kissing grew more intense, and his hand began to travel from my collarbone down to my chest.

"Wait," I murmured, placing a hand on his chest.

"I'm sorry," he said breathlessly, "you're just so fucking hot."

I inhaled sharply as sudden desire coursed through my veins.

"We just got here. I feel like we should wait," I whispered, staring longingly into his steely eyes.

He nodded and bent down to peck me on the lips. "You're right. I got carried away." He ran his hands down his face and smiled. "I can't believe we are here."

"I know! It feels so wrong and so right at the same time. I feel like a giddy little kid left home alone for the first time." I rolled over and propped myself up onto my elbow to face him. "How's Addison?" I realized immediately that bringing up his daughter was likely the best way to kill the mood. "Sorry, that's a weird thing to bring up right now."

"No, it's good," he said, propping himself up so we were eye to eye. "I like that you asked. She's good. I don't get to see her much, obviously, but I go over when she's with my mom."

I hadn't wanted to inquire too much about his personal life, but through my keen Facebook stalking detective skills, I'd determined that he had previously been in a relationship with Addie's mother, and at some point prior to him entering rehab it ended. His ex didn't post much on social media, but from what I'd seen, she was gorgeous. Annoyingly gorgeous. She had the brightest blue eyes I've ever seen and her face was perfectly proportioned, like a Barbie doll or something. It was a daily fight with myself not to compare, but it was hard. I still wasn't sure why he wanted to be with me. At best I was a seven, and he was like a twelve.

"When do I get to meet her?" I blurted. Kids had always loved me, and I knew that showing a willingness to meet his daughter would earn me some brownie points. At least . . . that's what I thought, but the face he made had me suddenly regretting the question.

"Um . . ." He hesitated, turning onto his back so he was facing the ceiling.

Shit, this was awkward. I had to fix it. "Not that I have to . . . I wasn't, like, assuming I was going to meet her. That's . . . What? Sorry."

"No, it's fine, you're fine. It's just . . ." He was trying to find a way to gently let me know he had no interest in me meeting her because he was going to sleep with me tonight and never talk to me again. Fuck my life.

I rolled onto my back to match his energy.

"I really like you," he began.

"It's okay." I wanted to stop him before he said it.

"I've kind of messed up the whole dad thing so far." He was back to facing me again. "And I'm trying to do things right. I really want you to be a part of my life, and I plan on keeping you in my life, but it's so new . . ."

"For sure. Yeah, no, I get it."

"I don't know what the future has in store, but the last thing I want to do is introduce her to someone who may not stick around for a while. I think it may confuse her, and . . ."

I had been so busy feeling defensive that I hadn't recognized that what he was saying was actually quite mature and sweet.

"It's not that I don't want you to stick around, it's . . ."

"I get it," I said, turning back to face him. "Seriously. I think it's wonderful. I've never dated someone with a child before, so I don't know how this works, but what you're saying makes total sense, and I absolutely respect it."

A relieved smile formed on his face, and he placed his hand on my hip. All of my senses heightened, and when he moved his arm, I smelled the warm woody, leather cologne he was wearing. He smelled like a lumberjack, and I couldn't take it anymore. I closed the distance between us and rolled on top of him. Our lips eagerly met, and his strong arms wrapped around me to pull me down closer. His hands found their way to the bottom of my shirt, and he gently tugged upward to remove it, then hastily tossed it to the side.

"Do you have a condom?" I whispered between kisses.

"Of course."

He flipped me effortlessly onto my back. My eyes fluttered as he sat up to remove his shirt, revealing his hard, muscular body. I'd never been with someone this physically fit before and suddenly felt intimidated. He paused for a moment, taking in the sight of my nearly naked frame beneath him. "You're so beautiful," he breathed, tracing his fingertips between my breasts, down to my navel as if he'd read my mind.

"Thanks," I said. "You too. Well, not beautiful . . . Handsome is what I meant."

His mouth curved into a smile as he leaned down slowly, kissing the area just below my belly button with direct eye contact. It left me completely breathless.

We both took off our pants, I closed my eyes and heard the condom wrapper crinkle. I probably should have kept my eyes closed, but I wanted to make sure he put it on. If I'm being honest, I mostly wanted to get a glimpse of what he was working with.

I must say, I was not disappointed.

The intense look on his face reminded me of a wolf about to devour its prey. I slid my hands around to his back as he lowered himself on top of me, letting out a gentle moan as our bodies became one.

His rhythm was slow and powerful as he pinned me to the bed with his hips. This was earth-shattering, this was life-changing, this was . . . *over*? He collapsed down onto me, his breath labored. My eyes popped open and darted around the room.

"I'm sorry," he huffed, rolling off me. "It's been a long time."

"No, it's okay. No worries," I said, pulling the blanket up to my chest.

"What the hell are you doing?" he asked suddenly.

"Huh?"

"Why are you covering up?"

"Oh . . . I just, I don't know. We were done so I . . ."

"What do you mean? We aren't done." He grinned, pulling the comforter down so hard it went flying.

My eyebrows lowered in confusion as he stood up from the bed and walked over to my side. He positioned himself between my legs on the bed and with both hands, slowly pushed them apart. I throbbed with anticipation as he lowered his face down between my legs.

Holy shit.

23

—

"WHATCHA THINKING ABOUT?" WILLA ASKED WHILE TWIRL-ing her crystal necklace around her finger.

I looked down and noticed—as always—she wasn't wearing shoes below her long, flowing skirt. "Oh, I was thinking about . . ."

"Colin," she said in a singsong voice.

My cheeks flushed. "Nooooooo," I said sarcastically, "I was thinking about stepwork and recovery, obviously."

Lies. I couldn't stop thinking about Colin's strong body pressed down against mine. I couldn't believe he hadn't disappeared after sex. And I couldn't believe how *different* sex felt now that I was sober. I was more self-conscious and exposed than the old days, when the drugs made me feel like a porn star.

"Mhmm." She pursed her lips and narrowed her eyes. "How have you been lately?"

"Really good. Colin is the sweetest, and he dropped flowers off on the porch for me yesterday," I gushed.

"No, I don't mean how are you and Colin, I mean how are *you*?"

"Oh." I leaned back into the chair and took a sip of my latte. "I'm great, really good."

She peered thoughtfully across the table at me for a moment, then exhaled. "Recovery-wise, how are you?" Her tone was beginning to sound accusatory, and I felt a ping of annoyance.

"It's fine . . . Why?"

"Well, it's just . . . I noticed you didn't bring any papers with you today, so I'm assuming you didn't finish your stepwork?" Her tone was passive-aggressive, which was one of my biggest pet peeves.

"Um, no, I didn't finish. But it's a lot—that step is a big step, and it takes time."

"I agree, it does. I could have helped you with some of it today if you'd brought it."

I took a breath to calm myself. "I'm sorry I didn't bring it. Next time."

"How's your dad?" She had changed the subject so quickly I'd nearly gotten whiplash.

"What?"

"Your dad, how's he doing?"

I studied her face as she pulled her chai tea up to her lips and took a gentle sip. She had such a warm, loving spirit, but today she seemed cold.

"He's fine. He's doing that experimental trial thing—it's like chemo in pill form and doesn't make your hair fall out or something. He seems to be doing all right." I shrugged.

She nodded. "When was the last time you saw him?"

What the hell was this, an interview? "Uh . . . geez, um. The night of Geo's graduation, I think. Why do you ask?"

"I'm concerned about you, that's all."

My heart began jackhammering in my chest, and my muscles tightened in defense. Why the hell was she acting like I'd done something wrong? Because I didn't bring my stepwork?

"Why the hell are you concerned about me? What did I do?"

"You didn't do anything." She gave me a reassuring smile. "It's what you *haven't* done. I'm afraid you haven't been working as hard on yourself as you can, that's all."

As realization set in, my anger grew. This was about Colin. She'd warned me it wasn't a good idea to get involved with him, and now she was desperate to prove she was right.

"Well, I disagree. I've been working really freakin' hard. I've been going to work every day, paying my rent, going to meetings . . . Like, what the hell." I glanced around the coffee shop to see if anyone had overheard our conversation. Being put in a position where I had to defend myself was aggravating. I hadn't felt this way since rehab, and it was bringing up old feelings of my disdain for authority figures.

Before she replied, I decided to dump out the rest of my thoughts. "I feel like you are going to say I'm distracted by Colin, and he's keeping me from growing in my recovery, but you'd be wrong. He's helping me. We go to meetings together, and he sends me encouraging messages all day long. He's made me happier than I've ever been, and being that you are one of two people who knows about us, it's kind of frustrating that you give off such negative vibes about him. I mean, just because I'm not out doing yoga all day under a tree, like you are . . ." I prepared myself for the inevitable argument we were about to have. I wasn't about to sit back and let her treat me like a stupid girl, too blind to see that a "boy was bad for me" or something.

The smile on her face surprised me.

"Thank you for sharing that with me," she said in her earthy zen tone.

"Don't . . . That's condescending," I replied.

"No, I'm not being sarcastic. I truly appreciate you expressing your thoughts and feelings. I mean the following with all due respect, okay? You tend to keep things surface level. I know you don't like confrontation, nor do you like talking about yourself. You just did both, and I appreciate seeing that."

My muscles relaxed slightly.

"I need to remind you that I am not your friend. I am your sponsor. That doesn't mean I don't like you; it just means that it isn't my job to sugarcoat things or idly sit by while you make decisions that might not be best for you."

I stopped myself from responding and continued to listen.

"I don't care about you and Colin; I care about you. I care about your recovery. You've been clean for a long time, but you've merely scratched the surface when it comes to living life drug-free. There is so much more to it than paying rent, working, and going to meetings. I want to help you get there, but I need you to help me help you. I'm not concerned about your relationship, I'm concerned about the fact that you haven't worked through the guilt and shame of your choices in the past. I'm concerned that you haven't learned how to regulate your emotions yet."

"Okay, first of all . . ."

"Hang on," she said calmly, holding up her hand. "And it isn't your fault. It isn't your fault you don't know these things, that's what I'm here for, to help you. And it happens through stepwork, which is why it's so important to me that you do it. Not because I'm a teacher giving you a grade, but because it's life or death."

I was listening intently, and the more she spoke, the more I understood. I could feel my defense mechanisms weakening as the understanding that she only wanted to help took hold.

"I want you to be 'the happiest you've ever been' because you made yourself happy, not because of someone else. If you give someone power over your emotions, then it's out of your hands and they can also make you the saddest you've ever been. Happiness comes from within you, not from a sexy boy. And he *is* sexy."

I chuckled. "I get what you're saying."

"Apart from Colin, are you truly happy with everything else? Like, if he wasn't in your life and you didn't know him, everything else—the job, the meetings, the house—does it make you happy?"

I closed my eyes to ponder the question. A knot formed in my throat and the sting of tears forming in my eyes gave Willa her answer.

"Sweetheart," she said softly, placing her hand on mine.

My chin quivered wildly, and all my feelings burst out at once. "I'm miserable, dude."

She gave an understanding nod.

"Like, what the fuck. It's so hard, like, just existing is hard. Waking up every day and not shoving a needle into my arm is hard. Having conversations is hard. Everything. I'm almost a year clean, and it feels pointless. I miss having a good time and partying. I miss having fun and doing risky shit. I miss my childhood, that feeling of innocence and shit. When my only worry was whether I got to be Mario or Luigi on the Super Nintendo. You know?"

Her hand was still on mine, and she hadn't stopped nodding.

"This shit is hard. I don't want to be a grownup. I don't want to have to make responsible choices and do the right thing and shit." I grabbed a napkin and hastily wiped my nose. "It's pointless."

"I get it, I really do. I was there, I promise. A life after addiction is hard, but it is so worth it. You have to get to the part where it becomes worth it, then you'll understand. This shit right here, this is the hard part, so you gotta do the work if you want the reward. And I swear to you, Tiffany, the rewards are beyond your wildest dreams."

I nodded, but I didn't believe her. The rewards she spoke of felt so far out of reach. I had so much work to do in order to "get my life back," and frankly, I didn't have the energy to do it.

As if reading my mind, Willa smiled and grabbed my hand. "If you forget everything else, just try and remember this—one day at a time."

I rolled my eyes. If I had a dollar for every damn time I'd heard this.

"I know, I know. But there's a reason these little slogans exist, okay?" She laughed. "As addicts, we get overwhelmed so easily. All you need to remember is, 'life is happening one day at a time.'"

I nodded.

"So tomorrow, what's the plan?" she asked, twirling her hair around her finger.

"Same shit: Go to my job, try not to call my drug dealer . . . maybe do some stepwork."

She nodded sympathetically. Maybe Willa was right. Colin had been consuming my thoughts, to the point that I'd found myself waiting around with bated breath for his texts. I wasn't focusing on bettering myself because I was too busy stalking his ex-girlfriends on social media and obsessing about our potential future together. I needed to shift my focus to myself, because I still had so much to learn.

I hugged Willa and assured her I would work hard to focus only on myself. Then, I decided to bury my head in my stepwork and only keep in contact with Colin occasionally. I would treat him like a bonus, hanging out with him at meetings but for the most part staying home and studying the steps. My one-year clean anniversary was coming up in a week and a half, and life was finally coming into focus.

That is, if nothing else distracted me.

24

I SHOOK MY HANDS TO DISPERSE SOME OF THE NERVOUS energy buzzing through me. Mary was standing at the podium in front of a hundred people, preparing to call me up on stage to receive my one-year medallion. It represented a year of keeping drugs out of my body, a year of doing whatever it took to avoid giving in to my primal urge to numb myself. I was so proud of myself and never for one second thought it would be possible for me, but here I was, still clean a year after my arrest.

"I'd like to congratulate my friend Tiffany on one year of sobriety," Mary said, beaming. The room filled with claps and cheers as I made my way up to the front to hug her.

"Thank you," I whispered.

"I'm so proud of you," she replied with a squeeze.

"Hi, everyone, I'm Tiffany and I'm an addict," I said, taking my place at the podium. "I know I'm supposed to get up here and tell you all how I did it, but honestly I have no friggin' clue."

A few people chuckled, and others shifted in their seats.

"Anyway, um. I got a sponsor and went to meetings every day, and if it weren't for other people in recovery, I wouldn't be standing here. Uh, but more importantly, I want to acknowledge someone else here with me tonight."

I quickly glanced at my sister, who was smiling and videotaping.

"I've known this man for a very long time," I began. "Since I was born, actually." I paused and heard my sister giggle. "I was in the darkest part of my life, and this man sent me a postcard every single day. He showed up for me when the rest of the world turned their backs. He told me during a jail visit that he'd received a diagnosis that meant he'd have to quit drinking if he wanted to prolong his life. And that's what he did. He began to work on his own recovery while I was still in jail. He loved me when I couldn't love myself, and he had faith in me when I didn't believe in myself. His unwavering love and confidence in me gave me the strength to keep going when death seemed like an easier option. It was crucial in me reaching out for help, and the only reason I'm here receiving this recognition tonight is because this man never gave up on me. This person also happens to have one year clean and sober, and I'd like to present this one-year medallion to my dad, Franky."

The room filled with raucous applause as my teary-eyed father pulled himself up with his cane and walked toward me. We embraced each other in front of everyone and sobbed in unison.

We did it . . . both of us. Together. We made it.

I was still high on the memory of that evening when I got home and sat down at the table in the garage for a cigarette.

"What you said about your father was beautiful." Mary smiled, and the other girls nodded in agreement.

"Your dad is awesome," added Toni.

"Tha . . ." I started to reply, but the room began to spin. I set my cigarette into the ashtray and gripped the edge of the table to steady myself.

"What's wrong?" Elyse asked.

I couldn't answer.

"You good?" Sam laughed, glancing around at the other girls.

I knew it was coming, and I didn't have time to stop it . . . I pushed myself back from the table, causing all the drinks on top to spill.

"What the f . . ." Toni started, but stopped midsentence when she looked back up at me.

I leaned to the side and covered my mouth, but it was too late. I was throwing up violently in front of everyone.

25

"I'M SORRY," I MUMBLED, GLANCING BACK TO SEE WHO WAS rubbing my back as I continued to heave. To my surprise it was my crabby older housemate, Tabitha.

"Here you go," she said. She handed me a can of ginger ale, then pulled the wastebasket from the corner over to my bed.

"Thank you."

"You're welcome. Let me know if you need anything," she said, heading to the door.

I nodded.

"One more thing . . ." She turned back to face me, then lowered her voice to a whisper. "I'd get a pregnancy test if I were you."

I gasped and opened my mouth to reply, but she'd already shut the door behind her.

How the hell did she know I'd had sex? Obviously I couldn't be pregnant, Colin and I had only done it once. Well, like six times, but it was all in the same night. Plus, we'd used protection.

But why did I get sick? I'd never experienced random nausea before. Didn't pregnant people puke in the mornings? This had happened at night.

The following day when Tommy dropped me home after work, I borrowed some money from Elyse, then walked to the dollar store. I was just going to get a test to get this thought out of my head. I'd just take it, and when it said negative, I'd stop obsessing.

Thoughts ran wild as I walked home. If I was pregnant, I would die. I would end it all. I couldn't have a kid, but none of the other options felt right to me either. I'd get kicked out of the house for lying and having a secret relationship. I wouldn't be able to do manual labor for Tommy anymore, so I'd be homeless and jobless.

No, being pregnant was not an option.

I let out a sigh and placed the pregnancy test between my legs. This was stupid, and a waste of time, but I needed to do this so my brain could shut the hell up. In three minutes I'd know and I could move on with my life.

"Miss you," I texted Colin while waiting for the result to pop up. I hadn't seen him in a few days and longed for his hugs. He had been spending time with his daughter, and, of course, I was unable to join as per our conversation. I wasn't jealous, I just . . . couldn't wait for the day we both had vehicles and real places to live and didn't have to be forced apart by our current circumstances.

"Miss you more, beautiful," he replied, along with a big-grinned selfie of him and Addie. She was so freakin' cute. I hoped she'd like me. If he ever let me meet her, that is.

It felt like three minutes had passed, so I set my phone on the edge of the bath and leaned over to check out the test.

A loud scream echoed through the bathroom, and it took a moment to realize the sound was coming from me.

I grabbed the test and dropped to my knees. This couldn't be happening.

I kept looking back and forth between the instruction pamphlet and the test, thinking there had to be a mistake. Maybe I was reading it wrong, or maybe it was faulty. It had to be, because there was no way in hell . . .

I was fucking pregnant.

26

—

"NO. NO . . . PLEASE, GOD, NO." I BEGAN TO SOB, HOLDING MY hand over my mouth to keep the others from hearing.

I had only been living in the halfway house for two months. Two friggin' months. *It's over,* I thought. *I ruined it, just like I ruin everything.* The room spun around me. This was all too much. I wasn't even supposed to be *talking* to Colin, let alone having his baby. NuStep had rules, simple ones: Go to a meeting every day, do your chores, make your bed, and don't have sex with meth addicts who live in other halfway houses and get pregnant . . . things like that.

My thoughts were spinning.

What the hell am I going to tell Mary?

Where will I go once they kick me out?

Maybe me and the baby could find a cozy dumpster to snuggle into. We could make it a home and the rats could be our pets.

God help me.

I had a year clean and so much left to learn about life without drugs. I had only just found out that you are supposed to put *two* sheets on your bed, not just the one. And that you must wait for the water to boil *before* putting noodles in. I was just beginning to learn how to be an adult and I could barely take care of myself, so how the *hell* was I supposed to take care of a baby? I imagined myself toting the baby back and forth across town on the bus and begging people for their spare change to buy diapers.

Can a baby eat cheeseburgers off the dollar menu?

A light tap on the door startled me, and I quickly began wiping my tears. "Just a sec!" I said, clutching the edge of the sink to pull myself up from the floor.

"You okay in there?" Sam asked through the crack.

"Yeah, I'm fine just, ya know, going to the bathroom . . . It's poop!"

Why . . . am I like this.

"Ew, could have done without that info," she replied.

I snatched the test and the wrappers from the counter, shoved them into my purse, and swung open the door. "It's all yours!" I said with a forced smile. Sam jokingly plugged her nose as she passed.

I shut the bedroom door behind me and leaned back onto it with my eyes closed. "What do I do, what do I do, what do I do?" I repeated to myself, hoping an answer would magically appear. I didn't know where I was going, but I was going. I left the house and began to walk. I needed to get as far away from other people as possible. I needed to talk to someone, but I was suddenly hyperaware that I had no one in my life I could talk to about this. Telling anyone at the house would put me at a huge risk for getting kicked out. My dad would probably have a heart attack.

Tommy would fire me, because who the hell wants a pregnant lady using a nailgun on a roof? Willa? I could talk to Willa, I guess, but the last thing I wanted was a lecture. Colin . . . My God, I couldn't talk to Colin. He could never know I was pregnant. He would freak out and leave me immediately. I wasn't even sure he knew my last name, to be honest.

There was only one person on the planet I could think of to contact about this, but the idea of having to tell this person about my situation made me want to die. But if anyone was going to lecture me, *then* scheme to come up with a plan, it was her.

"Son of a bitch," I huffed as I punched in her number, bracing myself for the inevitable lashing.

"Hello?" she answered.

Here goes nothing . . .

"You are an idiot." My sister's words shot through the earpiece of the phone and punched me in the side of the head.

I wanted to tell her to go eff herself. I wanted to scream and defend myself, but that's what the old me would have done. I would have shown up at her house and punched her in the throat.

"You're right," I agreed.

Silence.

"You're exactly right, I am an idiot. This was very stupid of me, I agree. But it's here and it's happening and there's nothing I can do to change it now, Laney. I'm terrified, and I don't know what to do."

"Have you told him?" she asked.

"No, dude, I just found out like four seconds ago. No one even knows we were talking."

"No shit."

"I'm freaking out."

She must have heard the tremble in my voice because she softened her tone.

"Oh, Tiffany . . ."

"What?!" I was still bracing for a lecture.

"Come over."

What?! My sister hadn't had me over since my arrest. I think she still had it in her head that I would steal something, which I probably would have a year ago.

"Really. Come to my house. I have a plan."

27

THE NEXT DAY, I STOOD ON COLIN'S DOORSTEP. I REACHED back to feel my pocket, ensuring the pregnancy test was still there. My fingers danced over the giant bow sticking out. Don't ask me how Laney convinced me to wrap it up and put a bow on it. She has always been very persistent.

I wiped my forehead sweat onto my sleeve, then walked up to the door and knocked.

"To what do I owe the pleasure?" Colin beamed, opening the screen door and leaning down for a kiss. He looked as handsome as ever, covered in sweat, screwdriver in hand. I wanted to jump on him right then, but we had business to tend to.

"Can you come outside for a sec?" I asked, glancing around nervously. This must have looked suspicious, because he started glancing around too.

"There's no one out here or anything," I reassured. "I was just . . . looking. Anyway, can you come . . . outside . . . for a sec." I smiled nervously.

He shot me a curious look as he stepped out onto the porch. "Shut that . . . Shut the door," I demanded with a forced smile.

"Why are you acting so strange?" He laughed, looking me up and down for clues. I'm surprised he didn't see the obnoxious green bow hanging from my butt.

My lips formed a tight line, and I took in the deepest of breaths . . .

"I feel like, you might wanna sit. Sit down or something. Have a little sit-ski . . ." *Stop talking*. I couldn't think of a good way to preface the bomb I was about to drop, so I reached into my back pocket and grabbed the box. I clutched it for a moment, then quickly shoved it into his lap, avoiding eye contact.

"What's this? Oh my gosh," he said, examining the Christmas wrapping paper. "You got me a present?" He relaxed a bit and smiled. "I think I know what it is," he said, nodding.

I bet you don't.

"Is it one of those fitness watches we were talking about the other day?! If so, you really shouldn't have. They are so expensive."

Well, shit. I'd forgotten all about that conversation. He had told me he wanted to start going to the gym and needed one of those step-counter watch things. How did I not realize this before . . . The shape of the box would fit a watch perfectly. *I'm so stupid.* My heart bounced against my ribs. This was backfiring. I knew the box was a bad idea and if my sister were here I'd drop-kick her in the eyeball. He'd gotten his hopes up and was going to be devastated once he realized instead of *a* watch, I'd gotten him something *to* watch . . . for the next eighteen years.

"It's not a watch," I blurted, smiling apologetically.

"Oh! It's not? I'm sorry, I shouldn't have . . . assumed. I feel like an ass."

"No, you're not an ass, I'm an ass."

"No, you're not! This is so sweet of you, don't feel like an ass. It means a lot." He leaned over and kissed my cheek.

I was frozen, unable to figure out how to make this stop. I watched from the corner of my eye as he slowly unwrapped the bow. I closed my eyes to brace for his reaction . . .

. . . and the sound of the front door swinging open made me snap them back open.

"What is she doing here?" I asked quietly, but it was drowned out by her shrill squeal.

"There you are, Daddy! I've been looking all over for you!" I stared wide-eyed as Addie ran out and hopped onto Colin's lap. "Who is *she*?" Addie asked, throwing her arms around his neck and hiding her face.

"I'm so sorry," I mouthed with a look of sheer panic. Colin smiled, seemingly unbothered.

"It's fine, relax. Addie, this is Tiffany, Daddy's friend. She came by to bring Daddy a present. You want to open it with me?"

"Yes!" she squealed.

"NO!" I bellowed, causing her to jump.

"Sorry . . . Addie, I'm sorry for yelling."

She looked me up and down and buried her face again. She hated me. I could tell.

"It's . . . You know what? This present, it's a grownup present and it's a teensy bit scary and, um, you know, I just . . . I don't want you to have a bad dream. But if you want, maybe we could get another present for your daddy sometime, that isn't, uh. Scary."

She moaned and nuzzled her head deeper.

Oh my God. What am I saying, what am I doing? I sounded like a psychopath. I wanted to dig a hole and jump in.

"Uh, okay, yeah." Colin hesitated in his unwrapping, seemingly confused. "Addie, honey, why don't you go inside. I'll be in soon." Addie didn't argue. She stood up and ran to the door, eager to get away from the creepy porch lady.

"I'm sorry. I'm so sorry. I wasn't prepared . . ."

"It's okay, Tiff, really. She is having a sleepover here. It's actually our first sleepover ever. Well, since she was a baby. You know what I mean. It's a big step."

"Whaaaaat?!" I whispered loudly, trying to sound excited. "That's . . . Wow. Good stuff, so cool . . . cool, cool, cool." I was trying really hard to hide the horror on my face.

"I think I'm going to enjoy being a dad, ya know? Like before, my priorities were messed up. I was sick, I was . . . *it was bad.* Drugs don't care if you have kids, they rip you away from your family and all the things that matter. But now . . . things are gonna be different this time, I can feel it."

"Yeah, for sure. So different, totally . . . hear ya on that. Um, *so.* Speaking of things being different. I . . ." I took a deep breath. "Here, let's just rip that Band-Aid off," I said, grabbing the box, tearing the paper off, and handing it back to him.

"Rip what now?" he asked.

"Just . . . open it. And I'm sorry in advance."

I heard him remove the lid, and I waited for his response. Silence. *He must be speechless, trying to find words not to hurt my feelings.* I slowly opened my eyes and looked over at him. He was staring at the test, unblinking.

"I just want you to know that there is no pressure here, okay.

We don't have anything to offer a baby, so it's like, I'm not, like, thrilled or anything. I know you already have your hands full with Addie and stuff, but I just . . . I just wanted you to know. And the box, the box was my sister's idea. She thought . . ."

"*Stop*," he said.

I choked on the rest of the sentence, careful not to let anything else slip out. He seemed angry; I was afraid to look.

"Stop," he repeated, softer this time.

I felt his hand fumble to find mine. He gave my hand a squeeze.

"Tiffany . . ." he began.

I looked up, and my heart dropped when I noticed the tears in his eyes. *Shit, I broke him.*

"Tiffany, this is the happiest day of my entire life." He gave my hand another squeeze.

I stared at him for what seemed like an eternity. It took me a minute to realize it was my turn to say something.

"Um, I'm sorry . . . What?"

"This is the happiest day of my life," he repeated, dropping the box and wrapping his arms around me.

I didn't reciprocate the hug because suddenly I felt terrified. This guy was a psychopath. I mean, he had to be. Right? What kind of person rejoices at the news that they've knocked up the pill-head down the street after only knowing her for two months? My mind was reeling. Part of me *wanted* to be rejected. I needed to be. I deserved to be. This was going way too smoothly. *Time to screw it up, Tiffany.*

"This is terrible news, Colin. In case you forgot, we are jobless, and technically homeless, and we are addicts. I had to ride a friggin' bicycle with a flat tire over here to tell you the news.

What am I gonna do, pop the baby into the basket on the front of my bike and tote her around town? Jingle a little bell to let people know we're coming through? Like, what the hell? We can't do this." I wasn't trying to be a bitch, I just had to lay out the facts, because apparently he was delirious from the shock of the news.

He smiled and inched closer to me. "Stop trying to push me away," he whispered. "I'm not going anywhere." His hand slid around to my back and he calmly pulled me into his chest. I pulled away.

"I don't get why you're acting like this," I snapped.

"Wait, I'm confused," he said, laughing and putting up his hand. "You wrapped this in reindeer Christmas paper, put a bow on it, and presented it like a gift, and now you're upset that I'm happy? What should I be doing right now? You tell me. Because I don't get it."

I stood up defensively and stared at him. "The wrapping paper . . . was stupid. Honestly, I don't know why I even . . . Listen, I'm concerned, okay. I just . . . I wasn't prepared for you to be happy about this. Of all the responses I've imagined in my head, joy was never included. I wasn't prepared, and now I'm a bit concerned, to be honest. I mean . . . what does this say about *you*?" I was talking to myself at this point. "I mean, tonight's the first night you'll sleep over with the kid you already have. The first sleepover. You don't even know if you'll like it. You don't even know what it takes to raise a kid, and yet you're excited to add another?"

"Ouch," he replied, setting the test down carefully beside him.

I snapped back to reality and realized he could hear all my internal dialogue. It's as if I'd forgotten he was here for a minute. I'd completely lost my grip on reality. "I'm so sorry," I said, dropping to my knees in front of him. "That was fucked up of me to say. I'm seriously sorry, I'm freaking out here."

"I get it," he answered softly. "I understand your worries, I do. And it sounds crazy and makes no sense, but I can't really put it into words, I just . . . I'm happy about this. It feels right, and if I've learned anything since getting clean, it's that God puts us in places that don't always make sense, but they are necessary steps toward a bigger picture."

I cringed. I was still on the fence about God, and I wasn't sure this had anything to do with him. Honestly, this felt more like the Devil's work. But he seemed so sure about this, so sure that everything would be okay, and for a moment . . . I felt safe, and somehow, I believed him. I faked a smile and nodded. He reached down and pulled me up onto his lap and held me. I could feel his heart beating quickly. I felt distant, like I was somewhere else, away from my body, trying to make sense of everything that was happening.

"I don't know what we are going to do, or how we are going to do it, but I say we just take this one day at a time, okay?" He looked up at me and the optimistic kindness in his eyes made me relax a bit.

The way he was gazing at me suddenly made something in my head click, and my blood ran cold. I jumped off his lap and took a step back.

"What now?" he laughed.

I studied his face carefully and shook my head. "Did you . . . did you wear a condom?"

He looked taken aback, and for the first time that night, he seemed angry.

"Um, yes? You watched me put it on."

I began to pace back and forth. "Yeah, I did. The first and second time . . . but after that . . ." My voice trailed off as I tried my hardest to recall the other times. I don't remember him putting one on after that.

"Tiffany . . . I know you're overwhelmed . . ."

"Just tell me!" I snapped, losing my grip on reality.

"I promise on Addie's life that I wore a condom every single time. I promise you."

"It was pitch-black once . . . The last time, there were no lights on, I couldn't see if you put one on, I just assumed . . ." I felt like a detective at the end of a crime show, on the precipice of solving the case, putting the pieces together, a picture of the event forming.

"Jesus, listen. There's no way to prove this to you, and that sucks . . . for me. But I can assure you that every single time my penis entered your vagina it was covered. I swear. I'm not an idiot."

"Well, how the hell am I pregnant then?"

"I don't know! You tell me! I'm trying to be cool about this and assume that I'm the only person you've been with, but how the hell do I know?"

Rage rose within me like a tide. "Are you fucking kidding me? You think I'm some kind of whore?!"

"What? I never said that! I just . . . This is getting out of hand. I think we need to take a breath together, okay. This is a lot to process, and I don't think either of us are very good at regulating our emotions yet."

"I can't believe you said that," I snapped.

He crossed his arms and raised an eyebrow, the corner of his mouth lifting into an amused grin.

"What's funny?" I demanded.

"Nothing is funny." He uncrossed his arms in defeat. "It's just, so far during this conversation you've basically accused me of not knowing how to be a parent, accosted me for being happy that you're pregnant, and implied that I sneakily and intentionally impregnated you, and I didn't react. But then the moment I questioned your part in it, you snapped."

I didn't know how to respond. My shoulders slumped and I shook my head. "I'm . . . I'm sorry. Fuck. You're right." He was so incredibly laid-back about this whole thing that I was finding it difficult to remain angry.

"Everything is going to be fine, I promise. I truly did use protection, so if a baby somehow managed to circumvent the latex barrier and make its way to your egg, I'm assuming it's a determined-ass baby. It's kind of demanding to be born. Who are we to get in its way?"

I laughed so loud I startled myself. He laughed too, and before I knew it, tears of laughter soaked my face.

"It's almost curfew," he whispered, kissing my forehead. "And Addie has probably been spying on us through the blinds since she went back in."

"What?!" I shrieked, pulling away and whipping my head around. The blinds were closed, and no one was there.

"I'm just kidding."

I smiled at him appreciatively, having developed a newfound respect for his levelheadedness. For a guy who used to do meth and rob department stores, he was really displaying some mature and responsible behaviors.

He pulled me close to him until our faces were an inch apart. His eyes bore deep into my soul and he gently placed his forehead against mine. "This is going to be good, I just . . . I can feel it. Try not to freak out, okay, and if you do, just call me. We are gonna figure this out together."

I nodded and gave him a kiss. Somewhere in the back of my head, alarms were going off over the fact he was being so wonderful about this, but I tuned them out.

"All right, I'm gonna go. I guess I'll make an appointment at a doctor's office or something. I'm not going to tell anyone until I figure out a backup plan for when they kick me out. I'll text you."

"We will make it work, don't stress. I'll talk to you soon."

"Okay, have a good night," I said, heading down the driveway. I picked up the bike from the lawn and threw my leg over, trying to look cool in case he was watching.

"Wait, one more thing!" he yelled.

I slammed on the brakes a little too hard and an awkward squeak escaped the bike.

"What, uh, what is it?" I asked.

He smiled at me, leaned out from behind the screen door, and threw his hands in the air.

"Let's get married!"

28

_____

ONE MONTH LATER

THE DOORS OF THE CHURCH CREAKED OPEN, AND FOR THE first time I was able to see the guests that had shown up for the ceremony. The pews squeaked as they turned to face me, all with looks of admiration on their faces. The music started, my cue to walk, and I took a deep breath, clutching the bouquet of daffodils in my hand. The music sounded off-key, slower than it should have been, but I ignored it and took a step forward. Even though I was staring straight ahead, I could see the crystals adorning my white dress, sparkling like little camera flashes beneath the church lights.

I glanced up at my father, who looked ten years younger, and I realized he hadn't brought his cane with him. I smiled and gripped his arm tighter as we took small steps toward the altar. I looked to my left and my right, smiling at all the faces I'd come to know over the years. Guests from my childhood, my adult life, former coworkers, and even a few I'd met in rehab. Everyone seemed so . . . proud.

I caught a glimpse of my mother. She flashed a satisfied smile as she dabbed away tears, careful not to smudge her mascara. She looked gorgeous in her sequined lace cocktail dress and I had to fight the urge to run and hug her. I mouthed "I love you" to her and continued toward my future husband.

Colin smiled and I noticed he too had been crying. I had never seen him wearing a suit, and he could have easily been a model for a bridal shop. I'd never felt more in love with him than I did at this moment.

Once we reached the altar, I hugged my father and turned to my bridesmaids. I passed the bouquet to Laney, who I'd obviously chosen to be my maid of honor. When I turned back to face Colin, I screamed out in terror.

It was no longer Colin standing in front of me.

It was Eliot.

"You stupid whore. You don't deserve a wedding. You don't deserve *anything* other than pain and sadness for what you did. Look at your mother, for God's sake—she's not even here," he growled. I turned to face my mother and screamed. Her face was no longer smiling and beautiful, it was now skeletal and gaunt, with pieces of flesh falling from the bone like a zombie.

"You destroyed my life," Eliot continued, "and now you have to suffer the consequences of your actions. Look around you, no one cares about you. You are nothing but a junkie loser and that's all you'll ever be."

I choked on my sobs and turned to face the crowd. The pews were now empty.

"Laney, help me!" I shrieked, turning to face my bridesmaids, but they were gone too. I spun to face Eliot and realized my sister was now standing beside him, her arms crossed and eyes black. "You destroyed us, Tiffany, and now we have to destroy you," he hissed, lunging toward me with supernatural speed.

My scream pierced through the night, and I shot straight up in bed. Elyse shrieked in response and jumped out of her bed.

"What! What? What happened?" she yelled in a panic, her face puffy from sleep. I could hear footsteps bounding down the hall, then the bedroom door swung open. The lights flicked on and it was only then that I realized where I was.

Covered in sweat, I stared in shock and confusion at the small crowd of women that had gathered outside the door. "I am so sorry," I mumbled, my voice raspy from sleep. "I must have . . . had a nightmare." My hand found its way up to my throat as I recalled the horrible images from my dream. Tabitha rolled her eyes and shuffled back to her bedroom. One by one the others headed back, some offering smiles of encouragement and others not saying a word.

Mary, with a look of sympathy, came and sat next to me, placing her hand on my leg. "Are you okay? Was it a drug dream?"

"I get those all the time." Elyse grumbled, before dropping back down into her bed and settling into the covers.

I felt humiliated. "I'm sorry, Elyse, I won't do that again," I whispered.

She mumbled something in response, but Mary tapped my knee. "Don't apologize, you didn't do it on purpose. You want to talk about it? We can go in the garage if you need a smoke." She'd never condoned my smoking before. She must have been able to feel how rattled I was.

"I can't. Er—I mean, I quit smoking."

"Oh wow, that's awesome, Tiff. I didn't even know you quit! You know, they say not to make any big life changes in the first year of recovery, so you don't overwhelm yourself. Quitting smoking is pretty big. I'm proud of you."

Smoking was nowhere near as big of a life change as the other one currently gestating.

"Thanks. I would like to talk, though, if you have a minute. There's something I want to tell you."

"Okay, sure, let's go." She smiled, but I sensed a hint of worry in her tone. I threw off the covers and followed her out of the room.

I hadn't planned on telling Mary about the pregnancy yet. I wanted to make sure I had enough cash stacked up first. I knew she would have to kick me out; a girl getting pregnant in a faith-based halfway house wasn't good for business.

It was getting to a point, however, where I wouldn't have a choice but to tell her. It had been nearly a month since I'd found out about the pregnancy, and a few days ago I'd had to have a tough conversation with Tommy and let him know I could no longer work for him. With all the climbing up ladders and inhaling paint fumes, the job was too dangerous, and I couldn't risk getting hurt. Instead of working, I'd spent my days trying to find another job so that there wouldn't be a lapse in income. So far, I'd had no luck. Same problems as before, with the only places willing to hire felons being gentlemen's clubs and bars, which clearly weren't options for me.

I hadn't told anyone other than my sister and Colin about the pregnancy. I hadn't even told my dad yet. I still wasn't sure how he'd take the news.

"Talk to me," Mary said as she took a seat on the couch. She kicked off her slippers and snuggled under a throw blanket. "What was your dream about?" I was still getting used to the idea that there were people out there who genuinely cared what I had to say.

I felt my palms start to sweat. "Mary, I want to tell you about my dream. But I can't. I have to tell you about some other things first. More important things. I don't know if it's because it's the middle of the night and I'm hoping you'd be less inclined to put me out in the street at this hour or what, but I just . . . I feel like I have to tell you now," I blurted, pulling a pillow onto my lap and hugging it.

Her face fell, and she made a *tsk* sound with her teeth. "No, Tiffany . . . Did you use?" She looked terrified. "Damn it, Tiff, please. Tell me you didn't use. I love you, but if you relapsed you know I have no choice. I can't risk you taking any of these other girls down with you. It's my job to protect—"

"No, Mary, I didn't. I didn't, I swear. I kinda want to right now, but . . ." She didn't laugh.

"Just kidding, it was a joke. I—" I took a deep breath, trying to find a good way to word it that made me sound less like a ho and more like a smart person who knew exactly what she was doing. It was impossible, so I just blurted it out.

"I'm pregnant."

The room fell silent. I swear, even the clock on the wall stopped ticking.

Mary's mouth dropped open and she froze like a statue.

29

—

"WITH A BABY," I CONTINUED, "A HUMAN BABY."

She didn't blink.

"That was weird. I don't know why I said it . . . like that. Anyway, yeah. So that's what's up . . . My HCG levels, apparently . . . are up." I laughed nervously. *Stop.*

"What the hell, Tiffany? What? How? Who . . . whose baby? When? I'm so confused." Her eyes darted, like she was searching around the room for answers to the question of when I could have possibly snuck off to fornicate.

"Colin," I mumbled incoherently.

"Huh? What did you say?"

"Colin," I repeated quickly and quietly, hoping she'd give up on the question.

"I literally don't know what you're saying. You're talking like you have marbles in your mouth."

I gave an exasperated sigh. "It's Colin's baby. Okay? Colin. The guy you caught me . . . making out with."

She threw herself into the back of the couch and crossed her arms. "You're kidding."

"I wish. Honestly, I wish it were a joke. I wish I could just chuckle and be like, 'Gotcha!' and go lay back down and wake up tomorrow fetus-free, but, somehow, this is real. And it's happening. And I'm . . . I'm sorry. I really am. Seriously, I never wanted this. I never expected it. We only did it once. Well, like six times, but in one night and—"

"When? Where? How?" She couldn't put the pieces together.

I closed my eyes in shame. "The overnight pass . . ." I was just throwing it all out on the table, fuck it.

"YOU LIED TO ME?" Realization about the extent of my betrayal crossed her face.

"I'm . . . I'm so sorry, Mary. I'm an idiot."

She stood up suddenly, and I jumped. She paced the room shaking her head. "I told you. I told you it wasn't a good idea. I told you it would be a distraction. I can't believe this."

I nodded silently, accepting whatever she had to throw at me.

"You . . . My God. You can't just . . ." She kept giving up halfway through her sentences.

"Okay, let's just take a minute here—"

"Tiffany . . . this is not good."

"Agreed."

"What are you gonna do? Does your dad know?"

"We are keeping it, and no. Not yet."

She sat back down and placed a hand on her throat, like she was trying to keep her soul from exiting her body.

"You're keeping it? Are you dating him? Have you been seeing him this whole time behind my back?"

I bit my lips closed and nodded.

She sat in silence for a moment. Possibly trying to find the right words, possibly trying to make sense of it all, but likely trying to refrain from yelling at me.

"I lied. And I'm sorry for it. I know I'm not supposed to live like that anymore and I've been trying really hard to learn how to be a good person and tell the truth and not manipulate. I messed up and let my fleshly desires get in the way of what God would want." I threw that last part in because God was like her best friend, and I knew mentioning him would get me some brownie points. Which was also probably a sin, and I was likely going straight to hell.

"And I'm a work in progress," I continued, "and I still have a way to go, but I lied. I wanted to be with him for an entire night. We hadn't done that. We're only able to see each other in bits and pieces at meetings or on bus rides and I just . . . wanted to sleep beside him."

"By beside him, do you mean on top of him?" she snapped. I pressed my lips together to keep from laughing. She didn't mean it as a joke, but it was hilarious.

"It wasn't the plan, I promise. I knew one thing would likely lead to another, but I swear I didn't think I'd be taking a parting gift with me after. I didn't think I'd get, you know," I said, gesturing toward my belly, "in one night."

"What are you going to do?" she repeated, perhaps hoping my answer would be different this time.

"I honestly . . . I think we are going to keep it and . . ." I paused once I saw her look of disappointment. I hated it. I was so used to that face. I'd seen it all my life. "Mary, there's something else . . ." I hesitated.

She clutched her heart. "Tiffany, I can't take anything else. What? What is it?"

I know none of this was funny, but her responses were cracking me up. Like a flustered mother hen.

"Mary, we are getting married."

I took the ring Colin gave me off my right hand and slipped it onto my left ring finger. "See?" I held it up to show her.

Colin hadn't officially proposed, but after that first night he suggested it, our conversations eventually evolved into the decision that this would be best for us. It sounded stupid saying it out loud, but both of us felt that the people in our lives would take us more seriously if we made this commitment. It was a huge risk, but one we were willing to take.

"What?" she gasped.

"Yeah, we are getting married. We are serious about doing what's right, and we know that if we are grown enough to make a baby, then we are grown enough to commit our lives to each other for the sake of the baby."

What the fuck am I saying? This sounded preposterous. What was I doing?

Mary stopped in her tracks. "Oh, Tiffany, you have no idea how happy this makes me. Oh, honey, I was so worried for your soul. You know having children out of wedlock is a sin, and when I heard you were pregnant, I mourned for you as I realized you'd have to live with this sin daily. Oh, thank the Lord you are doing the right thing. Come here, give me a hug, sweetie." She stood up and tiptoed over to me with her arms outstretched. I rolled my eyes, wanting to kick her in the kneecap for making this about God, but I settled for a hug instead.

She sat back down and began excitedly chattering about something, but my thoughts had trailed off. I couldn't get my mind off what she'd said about living in sin. I mean, I knew there was something greater than me out there, because if it were up to me, I'd be dead in a ditch somewhere with a needle stuck in my arm. But there was something keeping me from fully believing that I'd actually go to hell if we had this baby without getting married first. Now I didn't even want to marry him . . . out of spite.

I thought back to all the times someone said, "God had a plan, and that's why he needed your mother in heaven with him," or "Your mother is in a better place because she is with God now," and it made me want to scream. How the hell could being in another dimension somewhere in the clouds be better than down here with me and my sister? *We still needed her.* She was only forty-six years old when she died. We still needed her here, with us. If God was real, why was he slowly and painfully taking my father as well? Like, damn, you couldn't even leave us with one parent?

"You with me, Tiffany?" Mary asked.

"Yes, I'm sorry, I was daydreaming," I replied.

"Okay, so tomorrow we will just go over and explain the situation to Timothy, and I'm certain that once he hears your plan to marry, he will have no problem letting you stay. This is going to be great! What a true testament to the Lord. You are going to be the mother of the very first ever NuStep baby." She squeezed my hand.

Timothy was the owner of the halfway houses. "Awesome," I replied, trying to hide my sarcasm. I wish I hadn't zoned out. I missed a lot of what she'd said. Was she planning on making this kid a mascot or something?

"Okay, let's get some sleep, Tiff. We've got a big day tomorrow! By the way, when is the wedding?" she asked.

I smiled nervously . . .

"Next month."

30

"YOU GOTTA BE KIDDING ME! THIS IS GREAT NEWS!" DETEC-
tive Sealey said, rounding the desk to give me a hug. I made eye
contact with a Daffy Duck inflatable over her shoulder as she
hugged me.

This was my third visit with her, and I was a bit surprised by
her reaction. I'd been dreading it, actually. I thought for sure she'd
roll her eyes and tell me what a stupid mistake I was making, or
judge me for getting knocked up while having nothing to offer
the kid.

"Wow, how cool," she reiterated, taking a seat back at her
desk. She was the first person to genuinely seem excited for me.
There wasn't a hint of concern in her tone.

"I mean, I guess. It wasn't really my plan, but it's happening,
so . . ." I smiled nervously.

"Naw, it's good. Kids have a way of keeping us on track. Well,
for the most part : . . Anyway, you know if it's a boy or girl yet?"
She smiled, popping an Altoid into her mouth.

"Um, no . . . It's new. I'm only, like, seven weeks or something. So, yeah. It's exciting," I lied. None of this was exciting. The only feelings I'd experienced around this pregnancy were guilt, shame, and terror.

"It *is* exciting . . . I remember the first time I held my girl in my arms, I was scared shitless. I was in college and Dan, my husband, and I had no clue what we were doing. To be honest, I didn't even know if it would be possible to love someone other than myself. I was so focused on school and becoming a cop, I was worried that having a kid would deter me from my goals, you know."

I nodded. Minus the "wanting to become a cop" thing, the rest of it deeply resonated with me.

"But I'll tell you what, the minute I looked down at those beady little eyes and felt her little hand grab on to my finger, it was over. Nothing else mattered but her. I knew right then and there that she was the love of my life, and everything else was background noise. Luckily, I still accomplished my goals, obviously." She gestured around her office. "But it wouldn't have mattered if I hadn't, as long as I had her."

The wail escaping from my throat startled both of us.

I was open-mouth sobbing with abandon. The kind of a cry a kid makes if you take away their lollipop after they've already started licking it.

"Oh . . . shit," Detective Sealey said, jumping up from her desk and kneeling beside me.

Someone knocked lightly on the door and opened it. "Everything okay in here?" I didn't turn around.

"Everything is fine," she replied, rubbing my back, and I heard the door close again.

"I am pregnant!" I howled, my body jolting with each sob.

"Yes, you are," she replied, reaching for a box of tissues on her desk and placing them in my lap.

"I can't do this," I blubbered, blowing my nose loudly.

I could have sworn I heard her laugh.

"You can do this," she said calmly and confidently, "I promise."

I shook my head. "No, I can't." I sniffled. "I really can't. I don't have a job, I hate everyone, I don't have a car, my dad doesn't even know. It's all too much."

She took a seat back at her desk. "Look at me. Hey, look at me," she demanded. "None of that matters right now. Everything works out the way it's supposed to. I have tons of resources to help you. Okay. You're going to be okay. You aren't the first pregnant person to sit in that chair and you won't be the last. I've seen miracles happen for people like you. People in recovery who actually want a better life. You're all right."

"Why are you being so nice to me?" I squeaked, patting my face with a tissue.

"Because . . . you're a person. You deserve respect. That baby deserves a mom who understands that. You are not your past. You are not the choices you've made. You gotta realize that not everyone around you has ulterior motives. Okay? Chin up. You've been through harder things. Haven't you?"

I nodded reluctantly.

"Exactly. Now get up and piss in this cup."

My dad smiled as I approached the car after my appointment. "Did you pass?" he asked, as I sat down in the passenger seat.

"Surprisingly, yes," I joked, clicking my seatbelt into place. I turned to him when I noticed he wasn't moving the car. "You ready?" I asked.

Normally I'd take the bus here, but my dad offered to drive today. He'd never done that before, and it wasn't until I saw the expression on his face that it registered why he had.

"Dad . . ." I said nervously, bracing for whatever he had to tell me.

"The treatment isn't working," he said quietly.

His words were a punch in the gut. I swallowed hard and tried to remain strong. "Okay . . . What does that mean, exactly?" I was afraid I already knew the answer.

He shrugged. "I'm not sure yet, but hopefully it will involve some good-looking nurses."

I didn't laugh. He always tried to use humor to ease tension. I did too, so I knew exactly what he was doing. "Dad . . ." I said softly. His smile trembled. "Dad, I'm so sorry it didn't work."

He shook his head and frowned, trying to give the impression he wasn't bothered. "Hey," I said, placing my hand on his leg, "You don't have to pretend it's okay. It sucks, Dad, and it's okay to acknowledge that."

His chin quivered and his body eventually let loose with sobs. He made eye contact with me and I nodded as his true emotions finally broke free. I quickly unbuckled my seatbelt and leaned across the console to wrap my arms around him. As I felt his body trembling beneath me, I couldn't hold back my cries any longer and together we cried tears of helplessness and frustration.

"Dad," I whispered into his ear after some time.

He pulled away and we settled into our seats. He gave me a relieved smile and I knew he'd needed that moment just as badly as I did. We'd spent our whole lives covering all the meaningful things with jokes, and for the first time we allowed ourselves to just experience it.

"Yes, baby?" he replied.

"I know this probably isn't the best time to tell you this, but . . . I'm pregnant."

His eyebrows lifted in shock and he immediately broke down into sobs once again. Only this time, he was smiling.

31

I BURST THROUGH THE ENTRANCE OF THE RESTAURANT covered in sweat from jogging in the Florida heat. I had missed the bus and had no choice but to trek it. I must have looked like the Kool-Aid Man busting through the wall, because all at once everyone's eyes were on me as I dry-heaved and waved awkwardly, glancing around for a manager. I needed a job desperately to supplement my income. NuStep was being nice enough to let my pregnant ass live there despite breaking their rules, and I couldn't expect them to let me stay for free.

A woman wearing a white button-down blouse with loose bouncy curls made her way from behind the counter and over to me. *Bold move wearing white to work at a BBQ place,* I thought as she approached. "How can I help you?" she asked, her voice and bright and welcoming.

I noticed her name tag said "Manager," so I extended my hand and introduced myself. "I'm Tiffany. I am here for an interview. I know I'm late, but I can explain—"

"No, it's fine. I was a little late today myself. Come have a seat," she said, smacking the gum in her mouth and ushering me to follow her.

Mac's was a BBQ restaurant across town from where I lived, but Alannah told me they hired felons, so I decided to give it a shot. I had yet to make it to the "interview" portion of the hiring process, so to say I was nervous would be an understatement.

"Can I get you a drink?"

"No, thank you," I replied, trying to be polite, even though I would have given my right tit for a sip of water.

"I'm Claudia, I'm the general manager here. I was really impressed with your application," she said, looking through the stapled sheets of papers. My smile quickly faded. *Does she think I'm someone else?*

"Oh?" I inquired. I had no work history to report for the past two years, no references, and I'd checked off the "felon" box. "Impressive" wasn't a word I'd use to describe my application.

"Yes! I thought it was incredible how open and honest you were about your past. I'm in recovery myself, and I think it's great that you are working toward bettering yourself. When can you start?"

My jaw dropped open. I forgot how words work for a minute. "Umm . . . Oh. I mean, whenever you need. I can start."

"You sure?" she laughed.

"Yes, for sure. Sorry—to be honest I'm just . . . I wasn't expecting this. It's been tough trying to get hired, and I'm so used to rejection. I was just mentally preparing—I'm sorry, I'm making it weird, I tend to overshare. I—"

"I get it," she interrupted. "You're fine. As long as you show up on time and do the job, the past is the past."

"Wow, what a relief. That's awesome. Thank you so much." I couldn't believe this was real. I felt hopeful for the first time since I'd seen those two lines on the pregnancy test.

"Can you start tomorrow at noon?"

"Yes, for sure."

"Great, I'll see you then." We shook hands and stood up from the table, and as she walked away I suddenly remembered something.

"Wait!"

She stopped and turned around with a curious expression on her face.

I trotted up to her. "I'm so sorry, I forgot . . . to tell you something."

"Okay," she said, looking around nervously.

"I'm . . . I'm three months pregnant," I winced, realizing this was a potential deal-breaker.

She held out her fist, and I reluctantly gave her a fist bump. "Cool, me too." She smiled, then turned back around and disappeared into the kitchen.

"Have you talked to Eliot?" Colin asked, just as I was about to bite into my sandwich.

"What?" I asked, setting it down on the plate. The question felt like a punch in the gut.

"I just wondered. Now that all of this is going on with us, if . . . I don't know, you've reached out or anything." It didn't come across as a jealous pry, more like genuine curiosity.

"No, I haven't spoken with him. Not since the day of my arrest."

"What about his family?"

I shook my head. "Not since before the arrest. I came close once, back in rehab. Apparently his mother contacted my probation officer and said she wanted to be a part of my recovery and help me on my journey, but I . . . I declined. I wasn't ready, ya know? I still had so much guilt and shame about everything." I took a big bite of my sandwich. This pregnancy had me ravenous.

"So you never got closure or, like, a resolution. It's kind of open-ended."

I shook my head. "I mean . . . kind of, but not really. I'm paying restitution and I sent him an apology letter in jail. Plus Laney told me he has a girlfriend and is happy, so,"—I shrugged—"I don't know. One day I'd like to apologize, obviously, but I don't think now is the time. Can you imagine? 'Hey, sorry about our whole relationship being a lie and you finding out in front of your whole department . . . I'm getting married and having a baby and am super happy, but sorry about all that.'"

Colin nodded. "Yeah, I don't imagine that going over too well. I think that down the road, making amends is really going to help us. When we get clean there's all kinds of loose ends left over. We left a big mess behind, and acknowledging our part in it and apologizing will be good for us."

"Well, aren't you Captain Recovery-pants," I teased. "I can't believe I get to marry such a smart guy."

"I can't believe we're gonna be married soon," he said, shaking his head. "We're crazy."

"Agreed."

"You sure you wanna do this?" he asked, smiling mischievously.

The question caught me off guard. I knew he was joking, but for a split second I actually hesitated.

Am I sure? The wedding was only a few days away.

Is marrying a guy five months after meeting him as stupid as it sounds?

What if we do this and he relapses? Will I be a single mother?

We still haven't even told his mother. He wanted to wait until the last minute so she didn't try and lecture him out of it. I've only met her a few times. What if she hates me? I don't even know if she'll be a good grandmother to my kid.

I've only met his sisters once—what if they're bitches to me and treat my kid like an inconvenient mistake?

". . . Tiffany. I was just kidding, but you're making me nervous," Colin muttered, looking pained.

"What? No . . . I'm sorry, I just realized I left my wallet at home and got distracted," I lied.

"I'm paying anyway, so don't worry." He paused and locked his eyes on mine. "You sure you want to go through with this?" he repeated. It was no longer a lighthearted statement—he was now asking with concern.

I forced a smile and nodded. "Of course I am," I lied.

32

##

"I CAN'T BELIEVE YOU WAITED UNTIL THE MORNING OF YOUR wedding to figure out what the hell you were gonna walk down the aisle in. Why are you like this, Tiffany?" Laney asked, slamming her suitcase on the bed. She hastily unzipped it and threw open the lid, revealing the collection of dresses she'd pulled from her closet.

"I didn't even want to *wear* a dress, Laney. I hate dresses—you are the one pressuring me to wear one. I'm perfectly fine wearing jeans and flip-flops."

Of course I couldn't actually wear jeans, because they no longer fit. My clothes were becoming tighter by the day as my belly began to grow. We got lucky and had a beautiful sunny Florida winter day, neither too hot nor too cold. It was the perfect temperature to stand outside and marry someone who'd never seen me without eyeliner in front of a crowd of confused strangers.

"It's your wedding. You have to wear a dress, idiot. Now hurry up and pick one."

I sighed and began pulling dresses out one by one. I didn't own a dress myself. I'm not sure where they all went after my arrest. Eliot had given some of my stuff to my sister and a few things to my dad, and most likely burned the rest in a backyard ceremony while wishing death upon me.

I hated that this wedding was turning into a "thing." Colin and I had wanted to sneak off to the courthouse and get married. The idea of making a big deal about a wedding gave me a panic attack every time I thought about it. I don't like planning, I don't like hosting things, I don't like . . . *people.* I just wanted to do it and get it over with. Laney, however, had insisted that I would "regret" not having a ceremony and took it upon herself to plan this crap. I knew in my heart it wasn't true and I would have been perfectly fine without all the bells and whistles, but I'd learned that to keep the peace with my sister, sometimes I had to bite my tongue.

"This is the only long one, this one is fine," I said, holding up a purple and black dress I recognized from one of her high school dances.

She smiled.

"Do you think it's gonna fit me? I'm starting to get a little bump," I continued, rubbing my belly.

"Yes, it's big and flowy. It's perfect. Do you know what Colin is wearing?" she asked.

"I don't know. Hopefully not shorts, but I don't even care at this point," I said, pulling off my shirt. "This is becoming way more of an ordeal than I would have liked it to be." I could feel the anxiety beginning to cut off my air supply.

"What are you trying to say, Tiffany?" she asked, a hint of annoyance in her voice.

"Nothing, I just . . . wanted to do it at the courthouse. I just felt a little pressured into doing it in the backyard of—" I paused, realizing it was better to stop my sentence right there.

"Of Mom's house," she finished, "the house she loved, the house she would have wanted you to get married at." She adjusted the straps of my dress, not realizing it was so much more than that for me.

"I know she would have. But, like . . . his family is coming. Do you realize I haven't even met some of these people? Do you know how awkward that's gonna be? Like, 'Hi, everyone, welcome to my wedding, I'm the lady your brother knocked up, nice to meet you, sorry I don't have any hors d'oeuvres to offer you, I spent all my money on rent at the halfway house.'"

Laney gave me a playful slap.

"I'm serious . . . I don't think I can do this." I was basically gasping for breath at this point.

"You're doing it, Tiffany," she said, zipping up the back of my dress, "and who the hell cares what they think? It's your life."

I sat down on the bed and did some deep breathing exercises. I wish I could think that way. My sister was blunt and fearless. She never pretended to be something she wasn't and didn't give a damn what anyone thought of her. I, on the other hand, cared an insane amount about what others thought of me. In fact, it was my main concern in life. How others perceived me, whether I was offending them or hurting their feelings.

I didn't give a shit when I was getting high. I'd look you dead in the face and steal your wallet out of your purse without hesitation. Now that I was clean, suddenly everything mattered. I cared about things. Getting married in front of a group of disappointed strangers was one of them.

"If you really don't want to do this, I support you, and I'll sneak you out that window right there and we'll haul ass out of town."

I laughed, thinking about how many times I'd actually snuck out of that same window during my teen years.

"But if you do want to do this, then don't let your fear of these people stop you. You are marrying him, not his family. If worst comes to worst, you can have a perfectly good life without them. The kid will have me, and we already know I'm gonna be the coolest aunt anyway."

I wiped away a wayward tear. I placed my hand on her knee and she hugged me in response. "I love you, Laney."

"I love you too, and I'll always be here for you no matter what."

I nodded and took a deep breath.

"So what are we doing, wedding bells or prison break?"

"There are my beautiful daughters!" my dad exclaimed as we exited the bedroom. "Wow, you look stunning," he said, hugging me gently so as not to mess up my hair.

"Thanks, Dad," I said.

"Hey, that restraining order isn't still in place, is it?" he asked, glancing around nervously.

"The one for you or the one for Tiffany?" Laney replied, sending us all into hysterics.

"Believe it or not, there are no restraining orders against me for once, thank you very much," I said.

I was suddenly overcome with gratitude. For my family, keeping me grounded and laughing. I felt so fortunate that my dad was going to walk me down the aisle. I guess that was the one upside of getting married this quickly. My dad's cancer was aggressive, and had we waited a normal amount of time before getting hitched, he might not have been able to make it.

Ding-dong.

I accidentally screamed in response to the doorbell, and my sister's eyes grew wide. "Holy crap, it's them! We have to hide you! It's bad luck to see the bride before the wedding!" She grabbed me by the arm and pulled me back to the bedroom.

"Don't make it weird, dude. It's not that serious." I laughed, trying to keep up.

"Get in here and shut the hell up." She smirked, shoving me in and closing the door behind her.

I surveyed the room and noticed small pieces of tape clinging to the back of the door. I couldn't believe they were still there. I smiled, remembering all the photos of my friends that once hung there. I always thought we'd all be friends forever. I didn't talk to any of them anymore. Probably because they all went to college and became successful, and I decided to get drunk and do drugs.

Laney burst through the door. "Okay, everyone is seated. Are you ready?"

"Holy shit, I'm gonna throw up. Do they look mad? Are they miserable? I hate it here. I wanna leave."

"They look happy and proud, I promise. They brought gifts . . . You're fine," she reassured me.

I stared at her for a moment as anxiety tightened around my rib cage.

"Tiff . . . are you okay?" Her eyebrows lowered in concern.

I took a deep breath and shook my head. "I can't do this," I whispered as tears formed in my eyes.

33

—

EXACTLY FIVE PEOPLE WERE SEATED IN THE MISMATCHED chairs my father and sister had placed on the lawn. My sister had forbidden me from peeking out to see how they'd set up for the ceremony.

It took around five extra minutes for Laney to convince me to leave the bathroom and walk down the aisle. She said she supported me no matter what decision I made, but knew that my trepidation was likely due to fear. She reminded me that this day was about Colin and me, and the opinions of other people didn't matter.

She was right, but something just felt off.

My hands trembled as I looped my arm through my father's arm as we approached the aisle. My sister, who'd taken her place at the front of the aisle beneath the arch, smiled at me. Everyone, including Colin, who was standing beside her, turned to face me.

"What the fuck am I doing?" I whispered under my breath.

"Language," my dad replied, giving my hand a comforting pat.

There was no music playing as I made my way to the make-shift altar. We obviously couldn't afford musical equipment or a DJ, especially since the wedding planning began four days ago. I noticed someone had lined the walkway with garlands and faux flowers, which I recognized from my mother's Christmas decoration bin. I didn't mind that they had red and green lights weaved through the faux Aspen Spruce—I actually thought it was fitting. This is what it looks like when you decide to marry someone on a whim.

I smiled at Colin's family as I passed them, and they all mustered up smiles, but I could tell they were just as uncomfortable as I was. Addie was clutching a stuffed bunny rabbit, and she smiled and waved and I gave her a wink. We'd met a few times briefly, but I brought her a Princess Jasmine doll the second time we hung out and she'd clung to me ever since.

As we approached the front of the aisle, my father leaned down to whisper something into my ear. I braced myself, as I was certain he was going to remind me that it wasn't too late to run.

"I stole this arch from the church up the street," he said, pointing to the white wooden arbor above our heads. "I'm gonna return it when this is over, and I've already asked God for forgiveness."

I stifled a laugh, and used my bouquet to hide my face. He must have felt me rattling with fear and knew a joke would ease the tension currently pulling me toward the escape. He smiled, kissed my forehead, and stuck out his hand to shake Colin's. "I love you, man, congratulations," he said before taking his seat in the front. I stared back at my dad for a moment, trying to hold back the tears. I loved him so much. And clearly he loved me too, because he'd committed a felony for the sake of making my wedding look fancy.

I turned to Colin and faked a smile. He was wearing a button-down polo shirt with jeans and a pair of Nikes. Precisely what I'd expected him to wear. With shaky hands, I reached for his and took a deep breath.

I didn't know his family well enough to know what they might be thinking, but I imagined it involved embarrassment and confusion. I was thankful my sister was standing up there with us as the officiant, because if it weren't for her, I might have just hopped the fence and swum through the lake to escape.

Prior to the wedding she had asked if we wanted to write personal vows, and we both declined. I don't know why Colin had said no, but I know why I did. Each time I attempted to write them, I realized how *little* I knew about the man I was about to marry.

I hadn't yet eaten breakfast with him or seen if his laundry ever made it into the bin.

He had never seen me without makeup and was still blissfully unaware of how loudly I snored.

I had never even smelled a fart of his, which I feel is something that should be required before marrying someone.

I'd never even seen him angry before. What if he turned into a monster when he was mad and verbally or physically abused me? We would be married by then and it would be much more difficult to escape.

What the hell am I doing?

I thought I loved him, and had told him countless times that I did. But did I? *Could I?* Maybe I loved the idea of normalcy, and stability. Maybe I just loved the idea of love, and perhaps a wedding and child would show the world that I was no longer that worthless addict that everyone had written off as a lost cause.

Is that what I'm doing? Using a marriage to right my wrongs?

My sister had begun reading from the blue binder that my mother had used when she officiated weddings. I made eye contact with Colin and wondered what he was thinking at the moment. I could never read him. He was very level, never getting too happy or too sad. Never too excited or too depressed. He just rode the middle line when it came to emotions, so getting an idea of his thoughts from his facial expressions was impossible.

I squeezed his hands, and he squeezed mine. My sister was speaking, but I couldn't hear over the sound of my heartbeat and the loud voices screaming in my head. The voices telling me that his family was judging me and we looked foolish, on the brink of making the worst decision of our lives.

"Wedding rings are symbolic reminders of the unbroken circle of a healthy and abiding love. Within the safety and comfort of a true marriage, love freely given has no beginning and no end. Love freely given has no separate giver and receiver. Each of you gives your love to the other, and each of you receives love from the other. And the circle of love goes around and around. May these rings serve to remind you of the freedom and the power of your love," my sister recited.

This felt so wrong. Those words felt so permanent. I knew I wanted to be with Colin and have his child and be a family. I knew that—otherwise I wouldn't have been here. It just felt so . . . rushed.

"Okay, Colin, repeat after me: With this ring, I give you my promise to honor you, to be faithful to you, and to share my love and my life with you in all ways, always."

I smiled up at him as he repeated my sister's words and slid the wedding band onto my finger. We'd picked it out at a pawn shop together. We'd gotten his there as well. Together they cost a total of fifty dollars.

I repeated the same sentence and slid his ring onto his finger. I could hardly get it past the knuckle because I couldn't keep my hands still.

"Do you, Colin, take this woman to be your lawfully wedded wife, to live together in matrimony, to love her, comfort her, honor and keep her, in sickness and in health, in sorrow and in joy, to have and to hold, from this day forward, as long as you both shall live?"

I felt like I was going to pass out.

"I do," he said, smiling confidently.

"Do you, Tiffany . . ."

Oh shit. Here we go. It's happening. It's now or never. Oh God.

". . . take this man to be your lawfully wedded husband, to live together in matrimony, to love him, comfort him, honor and keep him, in sickness and in health, in sorrow and in joy, to have and to hold, from this day forward, as long as you both shall live?"

My expression became serious, and I gazed at Colin with pleading eyes, silently begging him to assure me that this was the right thing to do. It felt like an hour had passed, and I needed to say *something.* For the first time during the ceremony I glanced at the guests and made eye contact with my father. With tears in his eyes, he winked and nodded. "I do," I blurted, turning back to Colin. He jokingly wiped sweat from his brow and a few people laughed.

"By the power vested in me by the state of Florida, I now pronounce you husband and wife!"

Slow, halfhearted claps began and I turned to my sister and whispered, "Do we kiss now?"

"Yes! Crap, I forgot, you may kiss the bride!" she squealed, throwing her hands up in the air.

We laughed and gave each other a modest, simple kiss, then turned to everyone and waved. I tried my best not to make an apologetic face, even though that was how I was feeling.

Sorry for getting pregnant, sorry for making your brother marry me, sorry for forcing you to sit through this awkward ceremony, sorry for existing . . .

"Are you my mommy now?" Addie asked, making my heart drop to my knees. It was just one of the many questions I'd received after the wedding, including *Are you going to move in together? When will we know the sex of the baby? How will you guys get around town? Will you keep going to meetings?* I'd tried my best to answer all of them confidently, as if I were an expert in the field of shotgun weddings.

But Addie's question was on a whole different level of awkward.

"Nope," I answered, kneeling down to her (and her stuffed animal's) eye level. "You have a wonderful mommy already—I am just another person who gets to love you!"

"I don't need anyone else to love me," she whined, squeezing her rabbit harder.

"Addie, that's not ni—" Colin began.

"No, it's fine," I interrupted, smiling at her. "Okay! Well, how about you think of me as another grownup who gets to take you to do fun things like getting our nails done, going on picnics, maybe going to the moviiiiies. Fun girly stuff. I don't have to love you unless you want me to, and you never have to love me back unless you want to. Deal?"

She smiled and nodded, squeezing her rabbit tight. "Can we go to the movies now?" she exclaimed, jumping up and down.

"Not tonight, honey, it's a school night. But maybe this weekend," Colin said, scooping her up into his arms.

"Awwwww," she replied in disappointment.

"Who wants another burger?" my dad yelled, probably realizing he needed to rescue me. Because we didn't have much money for food, we'd picked up some burgers and hot dogs for the grill. Clearly, Dad was on to seconds.

Within an hour or so, people had started to leave.

"Thank you so much for coming," I said, giving Colin's mother a hug.

"Wouldn't miss it for the world. Let me know if you guys need anything, okay?"

"We will, thank you." I smiled.

"Great to see you guys," I said, waving to Colin's sisters and their husbands. "Thank you so much for coming."

They congratulated and hugged us, then made their way out the door, leaving only Colin, my sister, my dad, and me. I breathed my first sigh of relief in hours.

"Thank you so much, Laney." I wrapped my arms around her. "You did such a wonderful job."

"I'll send you an invoice," she said, giving my butt a smack.

"I love you, Dad. I'm so happy you were here." I gave him a big hug as well.

"Yeah, we really appreciate it. Sorry if my family seems . . . quiet." Colin shook my dad's hand and hugged Laney.

"To be fair," my dad said, "every family looks quiet compared to us."

"Ain't that the truth," Laney replied.

"So what are you guys doing now?" my dad asked, wrapping the burgers in tin foil.

"Well, we're jetting off to the Bahamas for a week-long honeymoon. Our flight leaves in an hour," I said, grabbing my purse from the chair.

Laney rolled her eyes and chuckled.

"Just kidding, we both have curfew, so we gotta be at our houses in like an hour," I said, wrapping my arm around Colin.

"Well, that's romantic. You guys need a ride back?"

"Yes, please." I smiled, thankful we didn't have to take the bus. Getting married and not being able to spend the night with your partner was heartbreaking, but I'd been banned from getting overnight passes ever since . . . you know what.

We got in the car, and Colin leaned over in the backseat toward me. "I can't believe we're married." He kissed my cheek and placed his hand on my thigh.

"I can't believe it either. I'm a wife. That feels weird to say. And I can't believe we're having a baby. It's crazy."

"I know, it's wild, but there's no one else I'd rather be doing it with." He squeezed my leg and looked out the window. I stared at the back of my new husband's head. I had a husband, and we were being taxied by my father because neither of us had a car. In all the times I'd pictured my wedding as a child, it was never anything like this.

"We're gonna be okay, right?" I whispered.

He turned to me with the kindest look in his eyes and grabbed my hand tight. "Hell yeah we are. We are gonna be better than okay. We're gonna be amazing."

I smiled back and nodded. He pulled me closer until my head was leaning down on his shoulder, and my smile immediately faded.

I realized that we were both pretending that this was perfectly normal and that everything was going to be beautiful and easy. The truth was that neither of us had the slightest clue what the future had in store. But we were hopeful. And sometimes, if you have nothing else . . . hope is enough.

PART
TWO

34

PRESENT DAY

"HOW DID YOU FUCK UP?" I ASKED MY HUSBAND. "DID YOU use?" I tried my best to keep my voice steady. I didn't want him to know that my fears were like a knife in my side, turning more and more with each confession.

"I relapsed, Tiff," he said, and my stomach sank. This was it. The thing I'd told myself would never happen in a million years had just . . . happened.

Colin went down the list of all the ways he relapsed, and I could physically feel life as I knew it shattering into a million little pieces. I blinked away a few tears as he continued, and fought with everything in me to hide the shock and horror I was experiencing. I didn't want him to stop confessing—I wanted to hear all of it.

"I'm so sorry, babe, I know I fucked up."

I nodded, then looked over at Marilyn. Her eyes were wide, and I could feel her silent shock from across the room.

"What about women?" I asked, matter-of-factly.

"What about them?"

"Did you hook up with anyone?" I braced myself for his response.

"No, of course not. Ew, no. It was just drugs, I promise."

"Yeah, it was . . . fucking *all* of them," I said, acknowledging the number of different substances my husband with ten years of sobriety had just shoved into his system. I didn't know what else to say; I couldn't process all this while staring at his stupid face. "Well, thank you so much for telling me the truth," I said, forcing a smile and wiping away another tear. "I'll talk to you later, okay?" I needed to be off the phone with him, because I couldn't hold back the flood of emotions any longer.

"I'm so sorry, Tiffany—"

"It's fine, we will talk soon, please be careful."

"I will. I love y—"

Click. I hung up the phone and dropped it, then collapsed to my knees as visceral, animalistic howls of agony and heartache escaped my throat.

"Oh, sweetie, I've got you!" Marilyn ran toward me and looped her arms under my armpits in an attempt to lift me up. I fought against it and sank further into the floor.

"I knew it," I sobbed, "I knew it, I fucking knew it. Oh my God, Marilyn." She had joined me on the floor and was rubbing my back. "I can't believe it, I can't believe it. What the fuck am I supposed to do? What are we gonna do? My kids . . . Oh my God, my poor babies. Why . . . why weren't we enough?" I sobbed.

"I don't know," Marilyn answered, even though the question

wasn't really aimed at her. "But just breathe. I've got you. Should we call your sponsor?"

"I would, but she relapsed last week after fourteen years. Because apparently everybody I love chooses drugs over everything. No matter how good their fucking lives are."

That's right. Willa had relapsed. My parents were gone. My husband was off doing God knows what. *What's the point of getting fucking close to people when they're just going to disappear?*

"You really cried the whole plane ride back to Florida?" Liz asked. After her relapse back when we were both in the halfway house, Liz had thankfully gone to rehab and returned to the house after I'd left. She and Elyse became roommates and friends, which was perfect, because they were basically the only two friends I'd made in recovery. Real friends, anyway.

Now she was sitting on my couch next to Elyse and Amber, the fiancée of Colin's best friend, the one whose Vegas trip was the scene of Colin's relapse. She'd been my friend since Colin and I had moved in together.

"Yup. Super awkward. The guy next to me was so uncomfortable, especially once I began oversharing the details of what my idiot husband did. He put his headphones on while I was in the middle of a sentence at one point, clearly tired of my shit."

Crying was nothing, though. I was surprised the four of us hadn't committed ourselves to a mental hospital. All our partners were pillars of the recovery community. Elyse was there for moral support; thankfully for her, her husband hadn't gone to Vegas. The rest of our partners had gone on this trip together and all of them had relapsed. They were supposed to have arrived home an hour before, but they hadn't. Now they weren't answering their phones. We were completely in the dark about what the hell was going on.

It was so surreal. I'd known these women for nearly ten years, and out of all the things we'd experienced together over the years—marriages, births, deaths, anniversaries—this was by far the craziest.

A small part of me was selfishly grateful I didn't have to experience this alone, but I still hated that we shared this pain.

"Still nothing?" Liz asked Amber. Amber shook her head. We were all deferring to Amber since technically her wedding was the reason we were in this mess.

"Steve said something about girls," Liz said suddenly.

My heart skipped a beat. "What?" I asked.

"Yeah, I don't know," she said, and sniffled. "Steve said the guys had girls up in the rooms or something. He didn't say who though."

"Did Colin?" I snapped. "Because he told me on the phone he hadn't screwed around."

"He didn't say who, like which guys. I don't know . . ." Her voice trailed off. Understandably. All of us were so defeated.

"Colin swore nothing happened with any women," I said again. "I'm telling you right now, the drug shit I can work with . . . If there were women, though, it's over."

Liz nodded. "For real, dude. FUCK these guys."

"Do you think they just didn't get on the plane?" Elyse asked the next night. Our husbands *still* hadn't come home. My friends and

I had moved past upset and jumped right into white-hot rage territory.

I shrugged. Then suddenly something hit me. "Oh my God, I'm so stupid!" I gasped, jumping up to grab my laptop.

"What?" Amber asked, taking a hit of her vape.

"The fucking bank account, dude," I answered, logging in to my online accounts.

"Oh, I already cut that shit off yesterday," Liz said.

"Dang, you could have told me, a-hole," I joked, knowing she probably forgot to tell me in the midst of her life falling apart.

My hand flew up to my mouth once I saw my bank account pop up, with a list of ATM transactions.

"Oh my God," I whispered.

"What is it?" the girls said, basically in unison.

"Since yesterday, Colin has taken out twelve thousand dollars."

35

"I'M GONNA MISS YOU, STUPID-FACE. CAN WE PLEASE KEEP in touch?" Elyse was crying like a baby as she hugged me good-bye. I cried too. Elyse was a true friend, and I'd miss our late-night shenanigans. But it was time to move out. I was pregnant and married and ready for the next step of our journey. I'd chosen to stay at the halfway house to finish learning everything I needed to know before being released to my own devices. Now that I was pregnant, I needed to ensure I was safe and ready. I didn't want to rush my freedom.

"Um, duh. You've basically been the father of my child this whole time, so I'm not just going to cut you out of his life," I joked.

She sobbed even harder. "I thought I'd lost you when you found out you were pregnant, you know that? I really thought Mary was going to toss you onto the street. So this is like losing you a second time."

"Thank you for everything," I said through tears. "Getting me water in the middle of the night, cussing out the girls for being too loud when I was trying to nap . . . everything. I love you." I gave her another big hug. Me and hugging were now getting along, unlike in the past.

I hugged Alannah, all ten pounds of her. I went to hug Tabitha, then remembered she hated physical affection, so I opted for a fist bump, and she obliged, then gave me a wink.

Toni had moved out and into an apartment with her daughter, Mikayla, the month before. She was thriving and happier than ever. I kept up with her life on Facebook, and it warmed my heart to see those two finally together. She worked so hard for this life, and she deserved every beautiful moment it had to offer.

Mary had tears in her eyes as she approached me, her arms outstretched. "Don't cry, Mary. I'm moving like four minutes down the road," I laughed.

She held me tight and rocked me. "I know, I know. But it's not the same. You are such a blessing to us, Tiffany, and I'm so happy for you."

"Mary, you are the blessing. I truly don't know what I would have done without your guidance and grace. You are an incredible house mother and I'm honored to have you in my life."

"You ready, punk?" my dad asked. He'd been leaning on the frame of the front door, watching the whole tearful, hug-filled goodbye scene.

I nodded and exhaled sharply. "Yes, I think so." I picked up the garbage bag of stuff I owned and looked at the women one last time. "All of you have helped shape me into the person I am today, and I'll be forever grateful for the memories we made here together."

Elyse let out a wail, and everyone laughed at her outward display of emotions. I tilted my head and smiled at her, then waved goodbye to everyone and headed off to my new life.

On the way to the car, my dad threw his arm around my shoulder. "You should be a public speaker—that was a beautiful exit speech."

I laughed. "No way, I have a phobia of public speaking. Thanks again for the ride, Dad. I can't wait until you see the new place!"

"Wow. This is . . ."

"I know . . . tiny, and empty. And it smells like rat feces, but listen."

"I was gonna say huge, luxurious, and smells like the Ritz-Carlton," my dad said. I gave him a gentle slap.

"Listen, it's sketchy, but we submitted like eighteen applications at fifty bucks a pop, and every single one was rejected. No one wants to let a couple of felons with no credit move into their place, so we weren't exactly in a position to be picky. But this is just a stepping stone to what comes next, you know? Rent is so cheap too. Only seven-fifty a month."

"That's awesome—how many square feet?"

"Seven-fifty—it's a dollar per square foot."

He nodded and surveyed the room.

"And there's a bus at the end of the street that goes right to my job. Well, it takes me to another stop where I have to get off and wait for the next bus that goes right to the restaurant. But it's a short walk compared to before."

"Did I see a police substation when we pulled in or am I imagining it?"

"Nope, you're not imagining it. You wanna see the rest of the apartment?"

"Sure," Dad answered.

The apartment was essentially falling apart at the seams. "It's not the greatest," I said, staring at a large hole in the wall, "but it's better than a jail cell, or rooming with another female." I was trying to convince myself. We were fortunate to have a place accept us, and I needed to focus on that. When I compared it to jail, it seemed like a palace. When I compared it to living with Eliot in a beautiful home with property and everything I could ever want in life, it seemed depressing. But I had put myself in this position, and these were the consequences. Besides, I'd rather live in a box with Colin, sober, than live in a nice home strung out on pills. This was going to be fine.

I stared at the mismatched couches in admiration. "I still can't believe the church donated all this furniture to us."

"Yeah, that's really cool. How did that happen?"

"Well, when my boss, Claudia, found out Colin and I were moving and starting over from scratch, she reached out to a friend who runs a nonprofit at their church. She told Debbie about our situation and . . . Yeah. They showed up with a freakin' U-haul full of stuff. Everything—lamps, pots and pans, you name it. Some guys brought all of it up the stairs for us and put it in here. They wouldn't even accept a tip."

"Amazing," Dad answered, smiling. "They must have seen how big you're getting and realized it's best to be nice to a pregnant lady."

"Ugh, tell me about it. Just a few more months to go," I replied, rubbing my belly.

"You need anything else before I head out? I can stay if you need help setting up or anything?" Dad said, leaning himself up against the door frame.

"No, thank you. I'm good."

"This neighborhood just makes me nervous. You sure you don't want me to hang until Colin gets home?"

Dad was such a worrywart. He followed my bus to school every morning when I first started kindergarten. He always wanted to make sure I was safe.

"I'm fiiiinnnne, Dad."

"You sure?"

A loud bang like a firecracker from outside made us jump, it was followed by another two: *bang, bang.*

I faked a smile, pretending not to know that they were gunshots. "I'm sure . . ."

36

—

"HEY, CAN YOU HELP ME PULL THIS SHEET ONTO THE BED? I can't reach it with my giant belly in the way," I laughed.

Silence.

"Babe?"

Nothing.

"Hello?!" I snapped.

"Huh, what's up, babe?" Colin looked up from his phone with a confused expression, like he'd just teleported here from another dimension.

The first few times he'd tuned me out, I laughed it off. But the closer I got to my delivery date, the less funny it became. "Can you put your phone down for a second?" I asked, taking a seat next to him on the couch.

"Sure, what's up?" He set it in his lap.

"Well, I'm freaking out a little bit. The baby is due in like a week, and we don't have his room set up. We don't have anything to put in said room, and after the stupid mandatory work meeting today, I am officially on maternity leave, which means no money is coming in."

"It's gonna be fine, babe."

I swallowed down my frustration. "Right, I hear you saying that . . . but I don't feel it. I don't feel like it's going to be okay. So I was hoping we could come up with a plan . . . together."

"Yeah, I mean, I'm not that stressed about it. Babies don't need much in the beginning, and I'm working overtime, so when my paycheck hits we will get some baby stuff."

I tapped the center of my forehead repeatedly with my finger, hoping it would knock a polite response to the front of my brain. "Okay, so when I tell you I'm stressed and you reply that you are not stressed, that is not helpful. In any way. Ever."

"I'm sorry—what can I do for you?" He scooched closer to me on the couch and put his arm around me. I allowed it.

"I don't know. I'm just freaking out."

"Well, have you called your sponsor?"

A wave of fury crashed through me, and I stood to my feet. "Are you . . . are you kidding me right now?"

"What? What did I do?"

I laughed, but not a funny ha-ha laugh. I let out a laugh that occurs seconds before someone's face gets ripped off.

"No, you know what? You're right. Why waste time talking to the man who put a baby in me about my concerns about said baby, when I can just call someone who collects butterflies and is basically in an exclusive relationship with the earth? Good idea!"

I snatched the keys from the holder and swung open the door. I didn't know where I was going, but I was sure as hell getting out of there.

.   .   .

I returned to the house a few hours later with only a Slurpee and some sanitary pads to catch the pee that escaped anytime I coughed. I wanted to avoid Colin, but he was sitting on the couch, smiling and staring at the door. It almost seemed like he was waiting for me.

"Hey, babe, we gotta talk about something," Colin said.

You're damn right we do.

"Um, okay so it's not bad. It's actually kind of good," he said.

I sat down at a dining room chair with my arms crossed and waited for him to finish. The only good news I was willing to accept was that he was on his way to buy stuff for this baby.

He exhaled. "Addie is coming to stay with us tonight, and probably for the whole weekend."

I shook my head slightly and blinked a few times. A million thoughts exploded in my head at once. *Why? Where will she sleep? There's no bed for her! Since when is she allowed to stay over? We have no food for her. We don't have cable for her to watch cartoons.*

"What?"

"Yeah, crazy, right? Her grandma called and asked if we could take her. Of course I said yes. I mean, this is huge, the fact they called and asked. I never thought I'd see the day they . . . Anyway. We gotta get stuff to decorate the room, like games and princess stuff. That way she feels at home, you know?"

Addie's grandmother had been taking care of her for a few months while Addie's mom got some affairs in order. I wondered if it had become too much work, taking care of a three-year-old. It's a lot of work for anyone, but especially a retired woman battling a sickness.

Anger spread through me. I tilted my head to the side and narrowed my eyes, "Okay, um . . . This is sudden." I glanced around the apartment, then back at him. "When you say decorate the room . . . you mean that one?" I asked, pointing to the spare bedroom I had assumed I'd be spending the evening turning into a nursery.

"Well, yeah. I mean . . . she needs her own space. We knew we'd have to figure out how to have both kids here eventually. We talked about that."

"Yeah . . . we did. But this was a far-off hypothetical future situation. I wasn't even sure it would happen when we lived here. I thought we'd get a bigger place after this with more bedrooms . . . I wasn't expecting . . ." I shook my head and stared at the ground in disbelief. I knew I should be happy and celebratory about this huge milestone, but all I could manage to feel was anger . . . and perhaps jealousy. This baby was coming any minute now. I'd just started maternity leave and was looking forward to resting. Now I had to decorate a princess room and watch a three-year-old?

"What about work tomorrow. Don't you have to work?" I asked.

"Of course."

He had gotten a job working on cars at a mechanic shop owned by one of our friends in recovery. The hours were long and he was gone most days until dusk.

"So . . . what are we going to do with her while you work?"

"What do you mean?" He laughed as if the question was preposterous. "I assumed you were going to watch her? She is your stepdaughter, you know."

I pressed my lips together and nodded slowly. I couldn't believe this was happening. We had just gotten into a fight over how stressed and behind I felt, and instead of helping me, he was plopping another child into my lap.

"I'm gonna go lie down," I muttered, leaning on the table for support and slowly pushing myself up.

"Wait, what? We have to get ready for Addie—she's coming in like an hour."

I nodded. "Go for it," I said, shutting the bedroom door behind me. I crawled into bed and pulled the covers up to my chin.

He swung the bedroom door open. "'Go for it'?" he repeated. "What the hell does that mean?"

My voice was calm. I no longer had the energy to give a shit about anything. "Are her grandparents planning on coming inside to check out the place? I hope not—it's a disaster. It would have been cool if we'd gotten a heads-up."

"Why are you being like this? I'm honestly shocked at how rude you're being. This is my daughter we are talking about. This is something I've been waiting years for. Instead of being happy for me you're being . . . I don't know. Nasty about it. What's your deal?"

"Just to clarify, Kaiden isn't going to have a room, correct? I just want to make sure we are on the same page. That's going to be a princess room, and Kaiden, our son, who you seem to have forgotten about, he's gonna sleep . . . what, in the living room? I just want to be sure I understand."

A look of fear and disgust crossed his face. I'd never seen him look that way before. "Okay, I see . . . So that's what this is about . . . Wow, you know, our son isn't even born yet and you are already playing favorites."

I wasn't looking in a mirror, but I'm pretty sure my eyes

turned red. "Are you . . . fucking kidding me right now?" I snapped.

"Look, I realize Addie isn't technically your daughter, but she is mine, and you are my wife. She is three years old, and that's three whole years I've mostly missed out on. Our son won't know if he's sleeping in a girl room or not—he will be a fucking newborn. I'm making this room special for Addie so she feels welcome. Because she is welcome. And if you don't like that . . ."

"What? If I don't like that . . . what, Colin? You gonna kick me out?"

He stared at me in disbelief for a moment, then silently exited the bedroom, pulling the door closed behind him.

I suddenly regretted marrying him. I regretted getting pregnant and moving in with him. I regretted getting clean and starting over. This was a mistake. I wasn't cut out to be a mother, and I definitely wasn't cut out to be a stepmother. Why the hell did I think I could handle all this?

37

I WOKE UP SOMETIME LATER TO THE SOUND OF A CHILD GIG-
gling. I must have fallen asleep. Laughter erupted again from the
living room and I realized that whether I liked it or not, my new
life as a pregnant stepmother had begun, and I had no choice but
to participate in it.

"Tiffy!" Addie squealed as I exited the room wiping sleep
from my eyes.

"Hi, honey," I mumbled, holding my arm out for a hug.

"Oh, your belly is getting big!" she said poking it. "Hi, brudder," she said in her sweet little voice.

"Ope, he just kicked! He must have heard you!" I joked, carefully avoiding eye contact with Colin. "I gotta pee—I'll be right
back." I patted her head and tiptoed to the bathroom. Sitting on
the toilet, I contemplated how rude it would be of me to go back
into the bedroom and shut the door. I didn't want to talk to Colin,
but I didn't want to ignore Addie, especially on her first night
with us alone.

I knew I had no choice but to be present, but I was void of energy and faking it seemed impossible.

I made my way to the sofa, ignoring Colin completely. I'd be damned if I was gonna be the first one to break the silence.

"Tiffany, guess what!" Addie exclaimed.

"What!" I said, matching her enthusiasm.

"Daddy said we had to wait for you to wake up, but now that you're awake we can start decorating my rooooooom." She did a happy dance and I faked a smile.

"Oh?" I said, staring only at her.

"Yep, yep, yep. And guess what?" she squealed.

"What?" I gasped to match her excitement.

"Daddy bought a crib and said we can put it in my room so I can help with brudder!"

I slowly turned to face Colin for confirmation. "You bought a crib?"

"I did. Hey, Addie, sweetie, I'm gonna put some cartoons on my phone. Can you do me a favor and go watch them in the other room so Tiff and I can have a quick chat?" He grinned at her and stuck his tongue out.

No, please don't go, Addie. I don't want to chat. I want to eat.

"Yup!" she said, jumping up and skipping to the bedroom. He followed her in and put Disney on for her. I wanted to run out the door and escape but figured that would be uncool. So I closed my eyes and took a deep breath to center myself. The baby was stretching my insides and it hurt to breathe.

"Listen, I want to apologize about the way I blew up earlier," he began. "At first I felt offended—it's been a big fear of mine that you wouldn't love Addie as much as you love Kaiden, and I guess when I saw the slightest hint of that earlier, I panicked."

I opened my mouth to speak, but he held up his hand.

"Just listen, please."

I let out an exaggerated sigh.

"You've been asking me to get stuff ready for Kaiden for weeks, and I keep pushing it off. It must have been confusing as hell to hear how quickly I was ready to jump at the idea of getting stuff for Addie. The truth is I'm scared. This is all new to me. When her grandma called and asked if I could take her tonight because her PopPop was sick, I was honored. She's never done that before. And the last thing I wanted was for Addie to get here and realize we have nothing for her, not even one toy."

My icy and defensive exterior began to melt away as he spoke.

"I just, I have a kid, but I haven't gotten to be a dad yet. And now my chance is here, and it's terrifying. I love you, and there's no one in the world I'd rather do this with. I'm sorry for not being more considerate of your position, and I promise to do more to help you during this pregnancy. Okay?"

My heart swelled, and I felt the weight of resentment fall from my chest. I was relieved and exhausted from this fight. I was thankful he was able to apologize for his part in this. I wasn't used to that.

"I'm sorry, too. If anyone should be sorry it's me. I was petty, and jealous, and my feelings were all over the place. You didn't deserve that, especially on such an exciting day. I promise to communicate better and not allow my pregnancy hormones to turn me into a psycho. I love you and am so happy you are getting the chance to be with Addie. I love both of you."

As we hugged, I breathed a sigh of relief. Holding all that anger was painful, and I was glad I got to release it. To top it off, I was actually pretty impressed with the way we handled our first fight.

Maybe I really *could* do this family / mom / wife thing . . .

38

"IT'S SHOWTIME!" MY SISTER YELLED, BOUNCING UP AND down on a yoga ball.

"I'm not even joking, Laney. If you say that one more time, I'm literally going to stab you in the neck with a scalpel."

I'd been in labor for nearly twenty-four hours. Kaiden had decided he wasn't in the mood to be born. The pain and exertion overwhelmed me to the point that I screamed like a banshee every time my uterus contracted.

"Please, listen. I know I said I couldn't have narcotics because I'm an addict . . . That was stupid. I shouldn't have said that. Please, I'm begging . . . Give me drugs."

The labor and delivery nurse leveled with me. "We don't give drugs for labor. However, as I mentioned earlier, we can get you an epidural, but you're running out of time. I need to know now if you want it."

"Yes, give it. Put it in me."

"Okay, I'll page the doctor."

It felt like hours passed before the epidural guy—aka the anesthesiologist—came strolling in with his cart. He explained the process to me, but I wasn't listening. He sat me up on the edge of the bed, and the nurse grabbed my arms to steady me. I glanced at Colin, who was staring at me with a look of terror on his face. The poor guy didn't know what to do. Also, he was probably horrified at the sight of me. I looked like an angry, bloated grizzly bear growling and thrashing around.

"Okay, I need you to stay very still no matter what happens, okay?" The nurse was looking directly into my eyes.

I nodded. "Just give it to me."

"I'm serious, you cannot move. He's putting the needle into your spine, so he needs you very still."

"I get it!" I screamed. "Sorry for yelling at you . . ."

She smiled. "I'm used to it."

"Okay, Mrs. Jenkins," the doctor began, "the needle is going in now." I closed my eyes and scrunched up my face in pain.

"Be still," the nurse reminded me.

"Very good, it's in. Now, just a reminder, epidurals aren't always one hundred percent effective. There's a chance you may feel only partial relief. Tell your nurse how you feel once we get this going."

"Okay," I said, wincing in pain. It felt like he was running a cable down the inside of my back.

"Now, this bag is a different mixture than we normally use, because you said you didn't want fentanyl in it."

"What?!" I yelped.

"Still, stay still." The nurse gripped my arms tight.

"I don't remember saying that. Let's switch it. I want the real one."

The doctor laughed. "It's too late for that, I'm afraid."

"It's not too late, we can do it . . . There's still time. Just pop some drugs in there and we . . ." I stopped midsentence as a warm, calming sensation washed over me from the stomach down. Suddenly, all the pain I'd been struggling with had disappeared. "Holy crap," I exclaimed.

"All right, go ahead and lie back. Carefully. Don't forget, you've got something sticking out of your back." The doctor began cleaning up his station.

I turned to him and smiled. "You're an angel. Thank you so freakin' much."

"I try. Leave me a positive review on Yelp."

I laughed for the first time in thirty hours. My sister gave me a thumbs-up, and I nodded. The epidural worked, and it felt amazing. For a little while, anyway. I'm not sure what exactly happened, but soon after the doctor left, I realized that the right side of my body felt great and the left side was burning with the heat of a thousand suns.

"Something is wrong. Only one side of my body is numb," I exclaimed after a few half contractions.

"That happens sometimes, hon. I'm sorry," the nurse said, not looking up from her computer.

The nurse walked out and I looked at Laney. "I'm gonna kick her in the teeth if she comes back in here."

"Do you want to play a game?" Laney was beaming.

"Do I want to play a *game*? Are you high?" I groaned as another contraction welled up inside me. "I feel like I have to poop," I moaned, squeezing the rail of the bed.

"I'm gonna go get the nurse, I'll be right back." Laney sprinted out of the room before I could stop her.

"You okay, baby?" Colin asked, walking over to me. He gently stroked my hair and leaned down for a kiss.

"Don't fucking touch me," I growled.

His eyes went round. "Holy . . . shit, okay. Sorry."

I howled like an animal. The pressure inside my body was tremendous. "Oh my God please, somebody help me! I want to die. Please somebody make it stop."

"I don't know what to do, I don't know what to do." Colin ran toward the bathroom, then swiveled on his heels and darted back to the chair. He stood there staring at the chair for a moment, then ran full-speed out into the hallway. It was like he woke up after having been in a coma for twelve years and realized he had legs. Suddenly, my sister reentered the room with an excited look on her face, closely followed by a nurse.

"Okay, honey, you feeling like you want to have a bowel movement?" she asked, snapping on a glove.

"I think so, I don't know. Maybe." I winced.

"Okay, I'm gonna take a quick peek, okay?" She stuck her fingers inside me. "Okay, give me a little push, honey."

I took a breath and pushed.

"Stop, stop, stop!" she yelled. "Okay, good. That's great." She took off her glove and ran to the wall to push a button before coming back down near my feet and placing a hand on my ankle. "You're doing great."

"Is it happening? Is he coming?" I asked in a panic. My teeth chattered and my body shook. I wasn't cold, so I didn't know why this was happening. "What's wrong with me?" I asked, feeling like I might vibrate off the bed.

"It's completely normal, Tiffany, just breathe," she said calmly.

I closed my eyes to breathe and a familiar voice made them snap back open.

"We ready to have a baby?" Dr. Stokes asked as he entered the room. He looked at the screen of the machine to check my contractions and looked back at me. "I think it's baby time."

"It's showtime," my sister whispered, giving me a wink.

I shook my head and laughed. "Somebody get me a scalpel."

Kaiden entered the world at 11:38 A.M. The moment they placed him on my chest, he peed all over it.

"Nice to meet you too, buddy," I whispered, stroking his sweet little head. I knew the doctor was doing something involving a needle and thread down in my lady parts, but I hardly noticed. I was fixated on this warm, wiggly little pink human. I wasn't sure what to do with my hands, so I laid them on top of his body, trying to cover as much surface as possible. I imagined he'd be cold. I had no way of knowing, of course—it was just a feeling I had.

"Would you like to cut the cord, Dad?" the doctor asked, handing Colin a pair of medical scissors. I looked over at my sister and noticed she was sobbing and sneakily taking pictures. The nurses said no photos, but my sister didn't agree and hid her phone in a bag of chips so just the camera was sticking out. They probably wondered why she was clutching Baked Lays and crying.

Colin took the scissors from the doctor, and as he cut into the cord, I found myself suddenly consumed with the idea that it was hurting the baby. "Does it hurt him?!" I screamed, louder than I intended. A nearby nurse placed her hand on my arm and shook her head. This child had only been alive for five seconds, and I was already prepared to punch his dad for taking a pair of scissors to him. I felt animalistically protective, which was a feeling I'd never experienced. I wasn't used to this many emotions, and if I wasn't so exhausted, I'd probably have a nervous breakdown.

The rest of the day felt like a fever dream. People kept coming in to check my vitals and give me paperwork. One lady even woke me up from a mini nap to try to sell me newborn pictures, and I think I told her to eat a bag of dicks. I do, however, remember my father entering the room while carrying cake and a balloon. I smiled up at him sleepily and pointed to the clear bassinet by my bed. His face turned red, and his chin quivered.

"Hey, little guy," he whispered, setting the cake down on the table.

"You can hold him if you want."

I watched as my dad gently lifted him up and held him to his chest. He took a seat in the chair by the door and stared down at Kaiden in admiration.

I thought back to the day he visited me in jail, when I'd been at my absolute lowest point. He'd told me he would always love me no matter what, and he believed in me and knew I could get clean. He wrote me postcards every single day offering love, support, and humor. I honestly believe that if it weren't for his unwavering love, Kaiden and I wouldn't be here today.

"Happy birthday, little buddy," he whispered to Kaiden, before looking up at me and smiling proudly. "And happy birth day to you, my beautiful daughter."

39

"AAAAAAHHHHH!"

Colin's scream jolted me awake. My eyes shot open, and I instantly panicked. "What? What is it?!" I yelled, sitting straight up.

"Don't move!" Colin had a look of fear in his eyes that made my heart stop. I looked down and saw one-month-old Kaiden sleeping peacefully next to me in his swaddle . . . and less than an inch from the edge of the bed.

I panicked and lunged for him, but Colin beat me to it.

"What the hell, Tiffany?" he hissed, picking Kaiden up from the bed. He slowly set him down into the crib and turned back to me with a disgusted expression on his face.

"I don't . . . I must have fallen asleep," I stammered.

"Obviously," he said, throwing up his hands. "If you'd coughed, he would have fallen off."

Guilt clutched my lungs, making it difficult to breathe. "I can't believe I did that . . . I was so tired, I didn't mean . . ." I covered my face with my hands, then broke down in sobs. I put my hands on my chest and used all my strength to draw in a breath. "I can't believe I did that!" I cried, waking Kaiden up. He began to wail, and I snapped into Mom mode and stood up from the bed.

Colin held out his hand. "Sit, relax. It's okay," he said softly.

"I'm so sorry," I replied, wiping away the tears and sniffling. I needed to make it up to him. I needed Colin to see that I was a good mother and that that was just a stupid mistake.

"Please, just sit," Colin said. "I'm sorry I got angry. Let me get the baby." He retrieved Kaiden from the crib and took a seat next to me on the bed. He studied my face. "I'm sorry, that just scared the shit out of me. I shouldn't have yelled at you."

I didn't respond. A tear traveled down my cheek and I quickly swiped it away.

"I should be helping more. You must be so tired. I'm . . . I can't imagine how tired you must be. This is my fault. I've been taking advantage of the situation. I just . . . I'm so tired from work, and you get to stay here all day, and I just felt . . ."

He stopped talking once he saw the rage cross my face. "I *get* to stay here all day? Are you fucking kidding me?"

"I . . . I meant . . ." he stammered.

I raised my eyebrows in shock. *"I get to stay here all day,"* I repeated, nodding incredulously.

"I'm sure it isn't easy, that's not what I meant . . ." Colin attempted to backtrack.

Without warning, all the unspoken words I'd held in for so long came spilling out at once. "I'm gonna be really honest here," I began, shaking my head. "You're right, it isn't easy. It's the hardest thing I've ever done. No offense or anything, but it definitely feels like I'm doing it alone. I've tried to be cool and make your life easy and make this a good experience for you so you don't regret accidentally knocking me up the first night we slept together, but I'm fucking done. I'm done pretending. I'm exhausted, I'm fat. My stomach looks like it was attacked by a cheetah, and my tits are giant, leaky friggin' watermelons. I feel like a cow with udders, and . . . and you . . ." I gestured toward him. "Well, you just look handsome as ever. You don't have twenty pounds of extra skin hanging off you or blood coming out of your vagina. You don't have hemorrhoids or tooth decay from calcium deficiency. Is your hair falling out in clumps?"

He gave me a blank stare.

"I didn't think so. How many times a day do you have to wash liquid poop out from under your fingernails? Probably never, right? I have a toothbrush under the sink for that very thing. After the tenth time of just using a washcloth, I realized a toothbrush would work better because it really gets under there. Anyway . . . yeah, so I don't get to stay here all day, I have no choice. Because I'm unable to work, physically, because I have stitches in my crotch and can't bend over without my rectum popping out. But if I could, I would. I'd love to have a few hours not hearing the deafening shrieks of our son. Or be able to go to the bathroom alone. Or have a grownup conversation. I haven't been able to get to a meeting in God knows how long, and to be honest, a stiff drink sounds really freakin' good right now . . ."

"Okay," he interrupted, "I get it. Jesus . . ."

"I don't think you do," I retorted.

"You're right, I don't. I'm sorry. This is all new. Why didn't you tell me you were so upset? Or ask for help or something. I would have helped you."

I shrugged, too tired to explain how I shouldn't *have* to ask for help.

"What can I do for you?"

I paused to ponder his question. I could think of a million things I needed right now. I needed a needle in my arm. I needed to get drunk. I needed a meeting. I needed to go back to jail, where everything was decided for me. I'd known it would be tough as a new mom but I'd had no clue just how . . . *lonely* it would be. "I need a hug, and a nap. And also ice cream . . ."

He laughed. "I've got the hug ready, but I have to go to work, honey."

"I know." I nodded.

"But I'll bring you the biggest tub of ice cream when I get off. And tonight, I want you to sleep. I'll take care of Kaiden."

I nodded and smiled. He'd forgotten that my boobs were required for the overnight shift, but I didn't want to ruin the moment. "Thank you," I muttered, giving a half-smile.

"I love you, Tiffany. We got this." He placed Kaiden in my arms and wrapped me up in a hug. "I'm stupid, okay? Just tell me what you need, and I'll do it."

"Okay," I mumbled into his chest. I was still angry, but now I had a bit of hope. Hope that I wouldn't feel so alone, and that we were in this together.

40

—

"OOPS, I'M SORRY, BUBBA, WAS THAT SCARY?" I LAUGHED. MY phone ringing had just startled five-month-old Kaiden. It was a number I didn't recognize, so I let it go to voicemail. *Probably another bill collector,* I thought.

Thirty seconds later, it rang again with the same number, and I cringed. I was trying to get Kaiden down for a nap and didn't feel like talking, but two calls in a row made me nervous. I decided to take my chances and answer.

"Hello?"

"Hi, um, yes, can I please speak with Tiffany Jenkins?" The voice on the other end of the line didn't say anything about the call being recorded, so I knew it wasn't a bill collector.

"This is she," I said, setting Kaiden's bottle down on the coffee table.

"Hi, Tiffany, this is Sal from the palliative care unit at Lakewood Medical Center."

"Okay . . ." I answered. I had no idea what "palliative" meant.

"We have your father, Frank Johnson, here, and I wanted to let you know that we are preparing to call in hospice," he said softly.

I sank into the couch, and the tears were instantaneous. "Should I come there now?" I asked, my voice cracking.

"I would say so, yes."

My heart thumped wildly. "Okay, where do I go?" I asked.

"Go to the front desk and give them your name. They will direct you to the fourth floor, okay?"

He gave me the address. I thanked him and hung up, tossing the phone next to me on the couch and burying my face in my hands. I'd dreaded this day, and it was finally here.

I thought back to the last time I'd seen my dad. I had mentioned to him that I was meeting someone from Facebook Marketplace to give them baby clothes that were too small for Kaiden. I'd told him where I was meeting the girl, and sure enough, when I pulled up, there he was, leaning up against his car, propping himself up with his cane. I shook my head and laughed before handing the girl her clothes and waving her off. Then I approached my dad and laughed.

"Seriously, Dad?"

"You betcha." He grinned. "I'm from New York. Meeting strangers in parking lots to exchange goods will get you killed."

"What were you gonna do, whack her in the head with your cane?" I laughed.

"If I had to, you're damn right," he replied, giving me a hug. "I'm glad you're safe, my baby. I gotta run."

"Wait, you came all the way over here just to watch me do this?"

"Hell yeah, and I'd do it again. I love you very much." He smiled and winked.

The day after the phone call, I stood next to the hospital bed and gazed down at my dad's face. I shook my head in disbelief that somehow his health had deteriorated so quickly he was no longer able to respond. I wiped the tears from my eyes and took his hand.

How did this happen? He was just fine the other day, I wondered.

Colin sat on a chair in the corner, playing with Kaiden and trying his best to keep him occupied. I imagined he was grateful having the baby there to distract him. It must have been uncomfortable for him to witness this.

Laney was there, as was my older sister, Jess, who'd flown down from New York by chance a few days before. Jess and I were ten years apart, and despite growing up in different states, we have a bond that I find difficult to explain to people. Some sort of sister telepathy. Once my knee began to ache out of the blue, and later that evening she called to tell me she'd been in an accident and injured her knee. She was also one of the first people who suspected I was getting high and hiding it. All the way in New York, she'd felt something was off.

There had been no change in Dad's condition since I'd gotten the call the day before. He was lying there peacefully, as if he were sleeping. Although I'd known this was coming for a while, I couldn't help but feel angry. I'd never be able to hear his voice again or laugh at one of his corny jokes. He'd never hold Kaiden in his arms again or look me in my eyes and tell me how proud he was of me. This was bullshit. Sitting around, just waiting for your favorite person to die. The person who made you, who raised you. The person you woke up to on Christmas mornings as a kid, who picked you up from school and tucked you in at night. It wasn't fair. My son would never know my mother or my father, and it felt like an incredible injustice.

"You okay?" Laney asked, taking a seat next to me and rubbing my back.

"Yeah, I'm just tired. I might go get a snack." I yawned and stretched, standing up from my seat.

"Why don't you go home? Take that baby home and get some rest?"

I shook my head. "I can't. I wanna be here when . . ."

"The guy said it could take hours or even days. He would want you to rest, you know that. I'll stay and will text you the minute anything changes."

"You swear?" I tried to hide the tears of guilt forming in my eyes.

"I swear," she whispered, giving me a hug.

"Do you mind if I have a quick minute alone with him?" I asked.

"Of course." She nodded, gesturing for everyone to leave the room. Colin was the last one out, and he shut the door behind him.

It was devastating and surreal to be in this position again, holding the hand of a parent who was about to leave me forever. As I looked down at his beautiful face, a lifetime of memories danced through my head. The time he built me and Laney princess beds. The way he would carry us down the stairs on his back in the morning before school and brush our hair while we watched cartoons. The way he made every single moment hilarious by cracking jokes and making silly faces.

I couldn't believe I'd never see those faces again.

Tears streamed down my face, and I gently ran my hand across his forehead. "Dad, I don't know if you can hear me, but I have a couple of things I want to say. If it weren't for you, I wouldn't be here today. I wouldn't have a family. It's because of you that my son has a mother, and I promise my children will always know who you are. I will never stop talking about you. Thank you for giving me life, Dad . . . both times."

I knelt down to give him a kiss on the forehead and lingered with my lips against his skin. Part of me hoped he'd pop up and say "Just kidding!" because that's something he'd certainly do.

Deep down, however, I knew he was already gone.

I closed my eyes and said a prayer. I prayed to whoever was listening that if my dad happened to go while I was gone, that they'd make sure he found his way safely to his next destination. I opened my eyes and stared at him for a moment, searching for the slightest sign of movement. "I love you, Dad. And I'll miss you more than you will ever know. Thank you for everything," I whispered. I quietly left the room and gently shut the door behind me.

Colin and I were fast asleep when we were awoken by the phone ringing at two A.M. It was Laney.

"Come back to the hospital now," she said.

Colin and I clattered through the halls of the hospital, me running while he carried a sleeping Kaiden in his carrier. We rounded the corner toward my father's hospital room and slowed down once we saw the nurse standing in the hallway outside his door.

As we approached, I knew by the look on his face that we were too late.

"He went very peacefully," he said.

41

"I'M SORRY, LITTLE BUDDY," I SAID, STARING INTO KAIDEN'S crib, where he was sleeping like an angel. It had only been a month since my dad had died, and I couldn't shake the thought that I knew exactly how my dad had felt all those times he tried to protect me. I understood what it was to love someone so passionately that the idea of them being sad makes you want to rip your heart out and give it to them.

That's why it killed me that I was about to change Kaiden's life forever, when he was still so tiny.

I flicked the light on in the bathroom and lifted up the pregnancy test one more time, just to triple-check that I hadn't read it wrong. Nothing had changed. It still read "Positive."

I covered my mouth to quiet the sobs and sat down on the edge of the bathtub to steady myself. I didn't even know that my lady parts were back up and running at this point, so I was in shock. I had *just* given birth to someone, and now I was going to be pregnant, nursing, or giving birth for two years straight. Besides that, if I was being honest with myself, I was struggling to maintain my sobriety. Every day was so stressful, and it made me want to just escape. Parenting was hard, marriage was hard, stepparenting was unspeakably hard, and not having my dad was crushing. More often than not, a pill to take the edge off sounded like a wonderful idea.

Before Colin got home from work, I composed myself and decided to try to make it fun. I was able to trick Colin into thinking it was a good idea to have a kid the first time with a little decorated box and bow. Why not surprise him again?

I grabbed a tube of puffy paint and wrote "#1 big brother" on the back of one of Kaiden's onesies. Colin was really into sports, so making a little jersey seemed cute. I finished wrapping it five minutes before he walked in the door from work.

"I got you a gift," I said, forcing a smile. Maybe if I seemed happy, he could find a way to be happy. I sat down next to him on the couch and handed it to him.

"Oh shit, is it our anniversary?" he teased.

"No, nerd. Open it."

He ripped open the wrapping paper and unfolded the onesie, holding it up in front of him. He didn't see the back. "It looks a little small for me. Maybe if I lose a few pounds . . ."

I gave him a playful slap. "Turn it around."

He flipped it around and his smile dropped instantly. He stared at the letters for what seemed like an eternity, then slowly turned to face me. "Are you serious?" he asked with a dazed look.

I nodded and laughed, then held up the test. He studied it, then gave me a fist bump and said, "I gotta pee."

My forehead creased. "That's it?" I was hoping he'd show more emotion, but I was starting to think he was incapable.

"I'm sorry, it's just shocking. I don't know what to say. I thought 'Awesome' might be a good start, then I realized you might take that the wrong way, so a fist bump seemed about right."

I rolled my eyes and stood up from the couch. Then I realized I had no room to judge his reaction. I'd cried when I found out, and they weren't tears of joy.

"I can't believe I'm pregnant again. Kaiden is brand-new. How the heck am I supposed to chase him around with a giant belly? And we have *no money*. This is crazy."

Colin paused. "It's gonna be awesome. They will be close in age and be best friends, you'll see. This is good, Tiff. It was meant to be."

It felt like he was reading from a script of "how to comfort your wife when you don't know how to feel emotions." I saw his effort and appreciated it, but I just didn't believe him. It didn't feel like everything would be okay. It felt like the beginning of everything falling apart.

"You're *joking*?!" Elyse gasped.

I was at lunch with Elyse and Liz, and I figured this would be the perfect time to share the news.

"I'm not joking. Twenty weeks as of yesterday. Isn't that nuts?"

"Why didn't you tell us sooner, asshole?" Liz demanded, plucking a tomato from her sandwich and tossing it onto the plate.

"The real question is, why would you order a BLT if you don't like tomatoes, you weirdo?" I snickered.

"Don't try to change the subject. I can't believe you didn't tell us sooner! We could have helped or something."

"Helped her what? Shave her legs?" Elyse laughed.

"No, I don't know. Helped her with Kaiden or something. It can't be easy chasing around a toddler with that belly." She pointed with her fork.

"Thank you, I appreciate the thought. It's definitely been . . . interesting. I didn't tell you guys because I just wanted to make sure everything was okay with the baby and stuff first. I don't know, I feel different this time. I got pregnant with her so quickly after . . ."

"HER?!" They screamed in unison. I glanced around the restaurant, and everyone was looking toward our table.

"Shhh." I was laughing. "Yes, we're having a girl."

"Oh my gosh, are you dyyyying? I've always wanted a little girl, you're so lucky!" Liz squealed. I tried matching her enthusiasm and faked a smile.

The truth is, I was actually scared. I was hoping for another boy. I know we aren't supposed to prefer one sex over another. It's just . . . I envisioned Kaiden and his little brother growing up together being best buds. Looking out for each other and stuff. I didn't know the first thing about being girly. All I ever saw online was photos of moms and their baby girls in matching outfits with bows and beaded sandals. I was gonna end up dressing my daughter like Adam Sandler. Colin didn't care what we were having, which was nice, but I'd secretly wondered if he did in fact have a slight preference.

This whole pregnancy felt different. It felt . . . off. I wasn't excited to be pregnant, and I didn't feel any connection to the baby inside me whatsoever. I felt like I should have by now. With Kaiden, it was instant. With her I felt . . . well, nothing.

"Yeah, I'm super excited," I lied.

42

"WE HAVE A BEAUTIFUL BABY GIRL! NINE POUNDS, WOW, she's a big girl!" the doctor announced proudly.

I stared at the ceiling feeling completely depleted. I felt the nurse place her on my chest and could sense my arms wrapping around her to stabilize her, but it felt automatic. My mind was somewhere far away, thinking about . . . nothing . . .

The voices in the room became distant and murmured. I reluctantly glanced down at the baby and began to sob. The nurse nodded and gave a slight smile. She must have assumed these were tears of joy.

They were tears of guilt and devastation.

"She's gorgeous, isn't she?" the nurse said sweetly. I nodded. The baby *was* beautiful, and she appeared perfectly healthy. Her blinking little eyes eventually found mine, and I started to cry even harder.

I am her mother, it is my job to love and care for and protect her, I said to myself. *So why is it that all I want to do is hand her to her father and beg him to never give her back to me?*

The next day, another nurse entered the room. She was holding a clipboard and tapping her foot. "We have to put something on the birth certificate. Have you guys decided yet?" It was her fourth time coming to the room to ask this same question.

"You pick," I said to Colin. I felt numb, but not in the way that drugs used to make me. A few years before, the numbness came with a payoff: euphoria. Now I was numb for no reason, and it was making me miss that high.

"Why are you not taking this more seriously?" Colin asked.

I didn't have an answer. I wanted more than anything to fawn over this precious new life. I wanted to adore her, and she deserved to be adored. I just didn't know how.

"I don't know," I said flatly. "I just want to go home. How about Chloe Faith?" I used to name my dolls Chloe when I was a kid, and I swore that if I ever had a daughter that's what she'd be called.

Colin stared at me like he wanted to kill me. "We talked about this before. That sounds like a Kardashian."

I didn't care. I was ready to leave.

As soon as we got home, the madness started. Two weeks later, it hadn't let up one bit. Chloe cried from the moment her eyes opened to the moment she shut them. Any attempts to soothe her failed, and eventually her shrieks became the soundtrack of my life. She was up every thirty minutes throughout the night, and her cries would wake up everyone, including Kaiden. Eventually I had no choice but to sleep in a separate room with her so the boys could sleep.

"Can I talk to you for a minute?" Colin had a concerned look on his face. He'd just returned home from work, and talking was the last thing I wanted to do. I wanted to throw the baby at him and run out the door.

We sat down at the kitchen table, and he grabbed my hand and squeezed it. He looked so happy and refreshed. I hated him for it.

"I know things are crazy right now," he began. I was hoping his next sentence would involve a massage he'd schedule for me, or a two-night-stay at a hotel alone. Any acknowledgment whatsoever about bags under my eyes or the knots forming in my hair would be nice. I was foolish enough to think that he paid close enough attention to me to realize I was at my breaking point. But I was sorely mistaken. His next words knocked the wind out of me.

"Addie is coming to live with us full-time."

My expression didn't change. I stared blankly as his words rattled around my brain, refusing to settle.

"You don't even want to know when?"

I didn't care.

"Anyway, now we have to enroll her in school soon, before she starts kindergarten."

I was looking at him, but there was no life behind my eyes. I was disassociating, lying somewhere on a tropical island with no children, and no husband. Just me.

"Tiff, did you hear me?"

I tried to focus my eyes. Chloe was screaming in the background somewhere, but I ignored it.

I nodded.

"Are you okay?" he asked, seemingly defensive. He must have expected me to squeal in delight and jump up and down. He was entirely unaware of the nail he'd just drilled into my coffin. Sure, down there somewhere I was thrilled for this milestone in their relationship. But it was too deep to reach at the moment.

I forced a smile and nodded, holding back tears. "That's really great."

"Well, yeah . . ." He wasn't convinced.

"I have to go get Chloe," I stammered, rising from the table and heading to the room. As I trudged the length of the hallway, reality finally set in . . . I no longer wanted to be a mother.

43

I COULD JUST RUN AWAY AND LEAVE ALL THIS BEHIND.

That little voice popped into my head one morning, and every day it grew louder.

Addie's school was forty minutes across town, so Colin and I woke up before sunrise every weekday, got the two babies out of their cribs—which were now in our room—and loaded all the kids into our single, solitary car. I'd drop Colin off at work, silently curse him for having the luxury to get away from all of this, and drop Addie off at school. When I got home, it was just me and the babies all day, listening to Mickey Mouse songs on repeat. If my friends called, I'd let it go to voicemail. If I filled up the tub, it would soon overflow because I'd forget about it. Besides, I couldn't hear the water over the sound of Chloe's constant cries. I'd taken her to the hospital countless times, and no one could figure out what her problem was.

I had no clue who I was anymore. I was an exhausted shell of a person, dead-eyed and going through the motions because I had no other choice but to forge ahead.

But what if I forge ahead right out the door . . . forever? I could go back to smoking blunts and selling pills, just me on my own.

One day, after returning home from dropping Addie off, Chloe started screaming the moment we entered the apartment. I pulled my breast from my bra and attempted to get her to latch on, but she was crying too hard. I looked over at Kaiden, who was in the corner plugging his ears. He hated the noise as much as I did.

"Stay here, kids," I said, setting Chloe down in her rocker and putting Kaiden in his playpen. "You'll be safe. Don't worry."

I realized I could fake some sort of kidnapping. If I could find a wooded area, I'd hide there for a while. I'd rather get eaten by a wild coyote than deal with another second of the screaming. People would think I was missing, and the police would start looking for me.

It all sounded so easy . . .

I picked up my phone from the couch, grabbed a hoodie and a bottle of water, and headed to the front door. I could hear Chloe and Kaiden crying, but I ignored it and shut the door behind me. I made it down the steps, realized I could hear their cries from outside, and fell to my knees, weeping. Part of me secretly hoped a neighbor would come find me so I could convince them to commit me. Three days alone in a padded room sounded like heaven.

The tears fell as I picked up my phone to call Colin to tell him I'd given up. Then, I thought of Toni. I'd wondered every day in NuStep how a mother could dare to use drugs after having kids, and now here I was, dreaming of abandoning my kids and getting high.

A photo of Kaiden holding Chloe popped up on my home screen, and I broke down all over again. How could I leave them?

I sprang up from the ground, ran back to our apartment, and picked up my phone.

"Garrison Obstetrics, how can I help you?" the receptionist chimed.

"Hi, um, I'm . . . this is Tiffany Jenkins," I said between sobs. "I don't want to be a mom anymore."

Not thirty minutes later, Kaiden was spinning in circles on the doctor's chair as we waited for Dr. Sullivan to enter. Normally I'd scold him for sitting there, but I didn't have the energy. Chloe shrieked from her carrier, and I just sat there, realizing that today was the first time since having children that I'd admitted I felt powerless.

Just like the first step in recovery, I suddenly realized. I was powerless over drugs *and* whatever was going on with my brain.

"I am so proud of you," Dr. Sullivan said, setting down his file on the table. "Mind if I sit there, buddy?" He smiled, and Kaiden jumped off the chair and into my lap. "You did the right thing coming in today, Tiffany. It takes a lot of bravery to do it. You aren't alone in these feelings. I believe you have something called postpartum depression. I'm going to ask you a few questions just to be sure, but the good news is, it's common, and we can fix it."

I instantly felt a weight lift from my shoulders. I had been carrying this shameful secret, terrified to speak about it for fear of being judged. I hadn't told Colin because I didn't want him to regret having kids with me, and I hadn't said a word to my friends because they all seemed thrilled about parenting. If I had known this was a common thing, and that I'd be welcomed with open arms instead of pitchforks and fire, I would have reached out a long time ago.

"In the past week, would you say you've felt happy all of the time, most of the time, not very often, or not at all?"

I paused and pretended to think, even though it was a no-brainer. "None of the time."

"Alrighty." He nodded and checked something on his paper.

Dr. Sullivan continued the line of questioning, and I answered each honestly. Hearing my responses out loud was depressing. How often do I cry? Every hour. Am I taking care of myself hygiene-wise? I haven't showered in eight days. Have I thought about hurting myself or others? Yes, I fantasize about driving my car into a pole at least once a week, because a month in the hospital sounds like a dream come true at this point.

By the end of the appointment, I had an official diagnosis: PPD. He also told me there were a few disorders associated with PPD, like postpartum anxiety, postpartum obsessive-compulsive disorder, postpartum PTSD, and postpartum psychosis. He explained there were millions of mothers across the country suffering in silence, reluctant to talk for fear of their children being taken away, and that this wasn't my fault. It was a rare form of depression that didn't discriminate.

"I'm going to write you a prescription for an antianxiety medication, and I want you to see a therapist as well. Having a real grownup to talk to is so important for parents. I mean, babies are great and all, but they're not the best listeners. Also, I'd suggest writing down or journaling some of these thoughts and feelings you've been experiencing. You aren't alone, and getting them out on paper is incredibly therapeutic. Maybe you could start a blog or something, my wife loves reading those." He laughed and then winked. "Oh, one more thing, you might want to see a GI specialist for your little one and ask about reflux. That screaming is deafening."

44

"KAIDEN, REMEMBER WHAT WE TALKED ABOUT," I WHIS-
pered, sitting him down on one of the hard plastic chairs in the
probation office while I set Chloe's carrier on the floor. I'd bribed
him with lollipops and a trip to the park after the appointment if
he behaved, but I knew I only had about thirty seconds before he
forgot all about the deal and transformed into the Tasmanian
Devil.

"Mommy, I gotta go potty!" he yelled, bouncing up and down
in his seat.

"Wait just a second, honey, they are going to take us back
soon," I said, desperately trying to fill out the paperwork that was
in front of me at check-in. The woman behind the window
scowled.

He hopped down off his chair and waddled over to the maga-
zine rack like a little drunk person. Then he started pulling the

magazines out and throwing them on the floor one by one. I put down my clipboard and rushed over to him, grabbing one from his death grip. "No, that is not how we treat things that don't belong to us," I whisper-yelled.

I looked over at Chloe, fully expecting her to make velociraptor noises while Kaiden copied her. Instead, she was cooing quietly. I still couldn't believe it. The GI specialist Dr. Sullivan recommended had diagnosed her with acid reflux, colic, and a dairy allergy, saying she must have cried so much because she was in constant pain. Ridden with guilt for not knowing that this smiley, happy baby was in there all along—and that I hadn't had the strength to fight to let her out—I jumped at the solution. I could do that now that my meds were working. I switched her formula that day, and miracles happened: She became a sweet, happy, smiling baby. I was basically obsessed with her. I was able to find that magic of motherhood that everyone spoke about, and our home—including Addie living with us—was running like a healthy, happy, well-oiled machine.

"Here you go!" I practically sang to the woman behind the window as I plopped my papers on the counter. "Last time you're ever going to see my pretty face, I hope."

More scowling.

Suddenly I heard a familiar voice. "Tiffany, come on back," Detective Sealey said, standing in the door of the waiting room. "How are you?" she continued as I tried to maneuver the baby carrier while simultaneously guiding my son into the hall with my leg.

"Amazing," I said, rolling my eyes. She laughed.

I sat down in the seat in front of her desk, and Kaiden ran right to the corner where her Mickey Mouse toys were. I smiled, remembering coming in here before I had children. I'd been totally confused by her choice of decor.

"You ready?" She smiled, looking through my file.

"Yup, let's do it."

"Here ya go." She handed me a cup. "I'll stay in here with these little angels and meet you in the hall when you're done."

"Sounds good," I said, grabbing it from her hand.

I went to the bathroom and peed into the cup. It was a dark yellow. *I really need to drink more water,* I thought to myself, pulling up my pants. Then I walked back into the hallway and knocked on Detective Sealey's door. She opened it.

"I think I already know how this is gonna go, but we gotta do it anyway," she said, smiling. She took the little test stick and dipped it into my swamp piss. After a few seconds, she set it down on the counter and waited. "You really need to drink more water."

I laughed.

"All right, just as I suspected, clean as a whistle." My heart leaped in anticipation of what was coming next. "Congratulations, my friend, all the conditions of your probation have officially been met. You are free . . ."

I smiled, and it quickly morphed into a cry. She reached out for a hug, knowing what a big moment this was for me. She held me and let me cry for a while, then patted my back and pulled away. I noticed she had tears in her eyes as well.

"I am so proud of you. You are going to do great things in this life. Keep up the good work, and please keep in touch." She shook my hand.

I had been on probation for three years, starting the day of my sentence. Once a month for three years, I'd walked, ridden a bus, borrowed a bike, or driven my car here. I'd shown up to this office, smiled at the receptionist knowing I wouldn't get a smile back, filled out the paperwork, and peed in a cup. Once a month for three years I sat across the desk from Detective Sealey sharing my fears, hopes, and dreams, absorbing whatever nuggets of wisdom she was willing to bestow upon me. Knowing I had to be accountable to her every month is part of what kept me on track with my sobriety. I hadn't considered until this moment that the only person I had to be accountable to now was just me.

My relief was suddenly tinged with fear.

I was on my own from here on out . . .

PART
THREE

45

I DON'T BELONG HERE.

Peering down the length of my new street, I was instantly reminded of a horror film I'd watched a few years back. A young couple in search of a home finds themselves in a suburban development where each house is completely identical. They end up trapped in a maze of homes that are exact replicas of theirs until they eventually get lost while trying to escape . . . and then they die.

So, basically, my life right now.

I'd taken the doctor's advice and begun writing. I wrote about my addiction and my time in jail. It started off as a blog, but when a mother reached out saying she wished her son in jail could read my writings, I knew I needed to write a book, something tangible.

I googled how to write a book, then how to format a book, and how to publish one. After eleven rejection letters from publishing companies, I decided to publish my damn self.

Somehow—and I'm still confused about how to this day—it became a bestseller. We shipped books to jails and rehabs all across the country, and I appeared on national TV shows. Someone from MTV called, asking to do a reality show about my family, and then a massive New York City publisher made me an offer to sell and market it. I started an Instagram account, filmed some videos, and went viral. My internet presence exploded. Apparently people thought I was relatable and funny. Money started rolling in and we bought our first home.

We'd hit the big time . . . or so I thought.

"Welcome to the neighborhood, I'm Brooke!" a voice behind me squeaked.

The neighborhood was packed to the brim with two-story single-family homes built with zero imagination. A few years ago I was eating green bologna in jail, and suddenly I was living in Pleasantville. Beautiful, successful, happy people were walking their adorable dogs and waving cheerfully to one another as they passed.

And apparently one of them was named Brooke.

I forced a smile and turned to see a startlingly gorgeous woman standing at the end of my driveway. Her long, shiny red hair seemed to catch the passing breeze and dance around her perfect face. I cringed for a split second, knowing good and well I looked like a swamp witch with strings of hair plastered to my forehead with sweat.

"Hi, I'm Tiffany, thank you so much! Do you live here?"

What a dumb-ass question.

"I do, yeah. Right next door, believe it or not." She smiled, nodding toward the house beside mine. My nostrils flared as an image of my husband and Malibu Barbie banging on top of her counters while I went out of town crossed my mind.

"Awesome! Very cool. It seems like a great neighborhood," I said, unsure of what my next line of dialogue should be in this awkwardly unexpected encounter. I had never been welcomed to a neighborhood before, definitely not by someone who looked like the prom queen at my high school.

"It *is* wonderful," she gushed, covering her heart with her hands. "Amazing families, wonderful school districts, and so many police officers live in here too, so it's super safe."

I coughed loudly in an attempt to cover my choke and smiled, trying my best not to look nervous. "That's really great news. I love the police. They're the best. They keep us so safe. I feel so safe."

Stop talking, Tiffany.

"So, listen! We're having cocktails down at Eighty-Six Hampshire if you'd like to join us. We leave the kids with the hubbys and have girly night on Thursdays, nothing fancy. I'm sure the women in the neighborhood would love to meet you," she chimed, pulling her sparkly phone from the pocket of her workout leggings.

I can't drink, I'm an alcoholic, I'll end up shooting drugs into my veins until I'm dead.

I can't say that.

"Thank you so much for the invite—we've got a ton of unpacking to do, though. Maybe some other time?" I offered. Did that sound rude? "Not that I don't want to come," I continued. "It sounds like a blasty blast. I love . . . girly time and . . . people, so much. It's just—"

"No! I totally get it. No worries, there are many weeks ahead of us, neighbor. Everyone in this neighborhood is so cool, and honestly, we've kind of become a little family. We are all trapped next to each other, after all. We might as well get along!" she laughed.

I tried to match her laugh to hide my panic. None of what she'd just said sounded fun to me. Friends, trapped, get along . . .

"Okay, I'm gonna get going. If you change your mind after you get settled, we will be down there—a drink might be nice after a long day like this," she said, smiling.

"I know, right!" I said a little too loudly. She waved and trotted off and once she was out of sight, I let out all the air I'd been holding tightly in my lungs.

I was sure that by the time their next girls' night rolled around, she would have already heard the truth about my past and be forced to revoke my invite out of fear and disgust.

I had begun to haul a box up toward the house when I noticed a large truck squeak to a halt in front of my house. Giant green letters on the side spelled "Johnny's Landscaping," and a man I could only assume to be Johnny hopped out of the driver's-side door.

"Hey there, are you Tiffany?" he asked, pulling a pair of gardening gloves from his back pocket. Behind him I noticed men climbing down from the back of the truck and pulling various tools and contraptions out with them.

"I am! Thanks so much for coming," I said, shifting the box of dishes to my other hip. I wanted to set this friggin' thing down.

"Great, I'm Johnny, but you can call me Peter," he said.

I laughed, then abruptly stopped once I realized that his serious expression didn't change. "Awesome, okay, cool. Nice to meet you . . . Peter."

"We have all the shrubs and plants you ordered. The only thing I couldn't get were the bellflowers, so I got irises instead. I know you said you were flexible and just wanted them to be purple. Irises are the closest thing and they are gorgeous."

"No problem! Do you need anything from me?" I asked, desperate to drop this box and not talk to another human for the rest of my life.

"Nope, you're good. We'll get right to it, Mrs. Jenkins."

Inside the house I began unpacking the dishes and setting them in the cabinets. My thoughts began to drift to how strange it was that there were landscapers in my front yard. Eight years ago, I was naked and writhing on the cold cement floor of a "suicide watch" cell at the county jail. Today I was paying people to put pretty plants in front of my pretty house in this pretty neighborhood in a depressing attempt to impress the pretty people.

Who the hell was I?

The truth was . . . I didn't give one single shit about flowers. I didn't even know what the hell a bellflower was. Johnny-Peter could have brought me a plastic plant and I'd have no clue.

This was good, though. I was giving my kids a beautiful two-story home to grow up in. Their father and I would be here every day to wake them up and tuck them in. We would use this blessing of a new life that we'd been given to ensure they didn't go down the same road as their parents did. Moving into this normal, cookie-cutter, family-filled neighborhood was a wonderful step. They would make the most amazing memories with their new friends here, and everything would be perfect . . .

That was, unless our charmingly affluent neighbors realized that two convicted felons with past burglary and firearms charges just moved in next door.

46

"THE KIDS ARE MAKING A FORT OUT OF THE EMPTY BOXES UP there. It's cute, I took a video for you," Colin said, smiling, as he entered the kitchen. His shirt was off, and all the efforts he'd been making at the gym were evident. *He was always at the gym. Twice a day.* His body was tight and muscular, not an inch of fat on him. I, on the other hand, hadn't seen the inside of a gym since 2004. He was officially way too hot for me. I was tired, overwhelmed, and overweight.

"Did you see the neighbor?" I scoffed, pulling another plate from the box.

"No, I haven't seen anybody yet. Why, are they weird?" he asked, taking a swig of water.

I wanted to make up a lie and say she had horrible breath or gonorrhea or something, but I realized that would be childish and petty.

"I don't know if she's weird, but she's a friggin' fox," I admitted.

"Wait, which house did you say she was in?" he asked jogging toward the door. "We're out of sugar, I'm gonna see if she has a cup," he joked.

I laughed and rolled my eyes.

"I only have eyes for you, darlin'," he said, running back to me and scooping me up into his arms. I cringed, feeling extra heavy and hideous.

Quick little footsteps running back and forth upstairs made me smile, forgetting all about my husband's nonexistent affair with the neighbor. The kids were running from room to room, giggling and exploring their new, much larger living space.

"You hear that?" I asked, pointing upstairs.

"Yeah, should we call an exterminator? What do you think it is, raccoons?"

I laughed.

"Mommy! Can we go play outside?" Kaiden squealed, bounding down the stairs with Chloe close behind.

"Umm . . . no, honey," I said, unsure. Colin frowned at me. "Okay, I guess so. Go on."

Colin and I followed the kids out the front door and watched as they raced across the street to join some other kids playing in a large grass space directly across from our house. Colin pulled down his tailgate, and we sat and watched the kids introduce themselves to the other kids and immediately become best friends.

As Chloe ran toward us, everything seemed to happen in a flash.

She didn't look before darting across the street. The car didn't have time to stop. I heard the squeal of the tires and the sound of something crunching. The world slowed down, and I opened my mouth to scream but no sound would come out. My legs were moving, but my mind wasn't attached. I saw her blond hair now tinted red, sticking out beneath the tire. Her sparkly sneaker caught the sunlight as it hit the ground with a thud ten feet in front of the car. The faster I ran, the further away she became. She wasn't crying, she wasn't screaming—the only sounds I could hear was the horrified murmurs of the driver as he exited the car and my heart pounding in my ears. Kaiden's little face was frozen in shock, staring down at something I couldn't see on the other side of the car. As I rounded the corner and took in the sight of my little girl on the ground, the scream finally escaped my throat . . .

47

"HEY!"

I turned to face my husband; he was wide-eyed with a look of confused panic on his face.

"What the hell, are you okay?" he asked, placing a hand on my shoulder.

My breathing was short and quick, and my heart felt like it would explode. I quickly turned to face the street and in the distance, could see Kaiden, Chloe, and the other children playing tag. Tears of relief filled my eyes and my face flushed with embarrassment.

I turned to face Colin. I wanted to apologize, but I couldn't catch my breath.

"You need to talk to someone, for real. This isn't normal," he said, shaking his head.

Ever since I'd gotten sober and had kids, I'd often have visions of them dying in all kinds of unimaginable ways. Recently, they'd become more frequent—and worse—and they were preventing me from doing the things I wanted with them. If I took them to play at the park, we'd leave after ten minutes because it became too overwhelming for me. At the county fair, when they ran too far ahead, I snapped at them. When they fell too far behind, I snapped at them. If they chewed their cotton candy too quickly or stood too close to a group of strangers—I snapped.

Most of the time, I was too afraid to leave the house with them.

Was this happening because I was finally happy with my life? I used to pray for death every day when I was on drugs, and now it had become my single greatest fear.

"You think I don't know that, Colin? You think I want this?"

"I don't know, it kinda seems like it. You're always on your computer working, and when you're not, you won't come out to do things with us because you are 'too afraid' the kids will get hurt. You get to stay home while I give our kids a damn childhood. Seems like you got it pretty good if you ask me."

I was incredulous. "Are you fucking kidding me?! I am with the kids all the time! I'm the one packing their backpacks and carting them to school. I'm shuttling them all over town to practices and dance class. Everything I do in this life is for them, so don't you dare say you are the only one giving them a childhood. You're on call at your job twenty-four hours a day, and gone all hours of the night. If you happen to arrive home in time to see the kids, you always need time to 'decompress.' I don't go to trampoline parks or carnivals or any of that other crazy shit you do, but I'm there for everything else, the things that matter most," I snapped, still grasping at any bit of air I could suck into my lungs.

"You need help, seriously. Like, this is getting out of hand. Do you think the kids don't noti—"

"Don't," I interrupted, holding up a finger to stop him. He exhaled sharply, sensing that if he pushed it any further there would be no turning back. He shook his head and went inside, slamming the door shut behind him.

I looked up, and there was our foxy next-door neighbor staring at me. Her mouth was wide open, and it wasn't just because she'd seen Colin without his shirt on.

48

"OKAY, TIFFANY, SO YOU'RE HERE BECAUSE YOU ARE HAVING dark and graphic thoughts, correct?"

My face flushed with embarrassment. It sounded crazy when he said it out loud.

"No . . . I mean . . . yes, I guess so," I replied.

I squirmed in my chair, painfully aware of how foolish it was to have made this appointment. Sure, I had seen a therapist for postpartum depression, but this was different. So I'd refused to take Colin's advice, but when Willa suggested I see a psychotherapist, I finally relented. Willa said she was ready and willing to help me with anything pertaining to recovery, but the things I'd shared with her were beyond her pay grade.

The therapist was probably going to take my children away and put me in a straitjacket. It wouldn't be the first time I'd worn one, and probably wouldn't be the last.

"I should probably also mention that I suffer from depression, generalized anxiety disorder, mild schizophrenia, and a few variations of OCD. I also have sleep apnea. I'm not even sure if that's related but figured I'd toss it out there," I joked.

He wasn't laughing.

Okay, Tiffany, reel it in.

"In all honesty, though," I said, "I'm an addict. Clean now—and have been for years—but I was addicted to pills for a while."

"Oooh . . ." the doctor said, and it was like a light went off. "Can you tell me a bit about these thoughts?"

"Dr. Lee, I just want you to know I came here on my own accord, okay? No one is forcing me to be here. I've been feeling a little off-center lately, but I'm a good mother. If anything, these . . . thoughts, they make me a better mother, because I'm more careful than other mothers," I said, trying my best to sound confident.

"I understand. What kind of thoughts are these? Are they violent thoughts?" he asked.

"Sometimes," I said quietly.

"Okay, how so?"

I looked down at his notepad, then back up at him. "So, basically, like if my kids want to go play outside or something, I say no. Which is especially hard to do because they hear the squeals of other kids playing out there. But I say no because the minute they ask it's like a projector clicks on in my mind and a horror film begins to play. Like in my mind, in my head, I can see it. It's real. I see my son laughing and kicking the ball in the yard, I see my daughter giggle and chasing after it, even as it rolls into the street. She's so innocent. She doesn't look. She's too excited to look," I said, my voice trailing off.

"Okay, Tiffany," Dr. Lee said gently, "that's enough for now. That's good. Take a breath."

I cried instead. I rarely cried anymore. My friends often joked that I was a sociopath. So I guess the doc could rule that one out at least. I snatched a tissue out of the box next to me and quickly dabbed away my tears.

"Tiffany, how long have you been having these thoughts?" he asked, cocking his head slightly.

I cleared my throat. "About my children, or thoughts like this in general?"

"No, just in general. Have you always had intrusive thoughts like this?"

"Um, yeah. I guess. Once I started having children it became less about me and more about them."

"What were they about when you were a child? Do you re-member any of them, the thoughts? Was it the same as it is now, like a movie playing?" he asked, readjusting his position in his seat.

"Not really. I guess maybe because when I was little, I hadn't really seen any, like, graphic images? So I didn't have any specific things to imagine. Not like now—my mind is filled with the hor-rors of today's world. I guess as I got older and the internet made it possible to look up crime scenes and the aftermath of car acci-dents and stuff, it made life seem more . . . I don't know, tempo-rary? I guess. Like there are a million ways for us to die each day, and the fact that we don't is a miracle, honestly."

"You have a good point, but let me switch gears here for a mo-ment. Do you like to ride roller coasters?" he asked.

"Ew, no, I'm old and will literally puke from the sky. I can't. No."

He laughed. "Okay, bad example—do you like horror mov-ies?"

I smiled, knowing exactly where he was going with this. If I said yes, he would correlate my love of horror films with these thoughts I've been having, and suggest I stop watching videos of people getting hacked up by a man in the woods if I wanted to feel better. But I decided to tell the truth.

"I do, actually, yes. It's my favorite genre, and it always has been, but that's not why I'm thinking about these things. For the record."

"Describe the feelings you have when watching a scary movie," he said, leaning back in his chair and placing his hands in his lap.

"Um . . . I feel scared, I guess. Nervous, maybe. Jumpy."

"So you must not mind all those feelings then," he said.

"No, not at all. I love it."

"Ahhh, I see. When it's convenient for you, I suppose."

"I'm sorry?" I asked, not understanding.

"You intentionally chose to watch horror movies, knowing and—according to you—enjoying that they make you feel frightened, jumpy, and nervous. You like feeling those things. Those feelings aren't bad . . . unless," he said, holding up his pen. I waited for him to finish, but I could tell by his face he was expecting me to fill in the blank. He reminded me of a mad scientist.

"Unless what?" I asked, genuinely having no idea what this dude was insinuating.

"Unless it happens at an inconvenient time. It's not the feeling of anxiety itself that's bad, it's that it doesn't match up with the moment or current level of danger."

I wasn't sure I was following.

"It's like turning on a light switch and suddenly being punched in the side of the head. Getting punched in the head has its place, like in a bar fight or in the UFC ring, but it's not supposed to happen when you turn on a light in your home. Same with those feelings of anxiety you experience day to day. They have their place—like when you watch a scary movie or ride a roller coaster, but they don't belong on the playground with you while you're enjoying time with your children. Does that make sense?"

Holy shit.

"Yes, actually. That makes a lot of sense," I said.

"To top it off, when you were using, you were covering up those thoughts and that anxiety with drugs. Now you're sober, and BOOM. All the feelings."

"Tell me about it," I sighed. "So how do I make it stop? Like, without drugs? I mean, the kind you shoot in your veins . . ."

He smiled. "You can learn to recognize the thoughts when they come, and have coping mechanisms in place for when they do. If you get to those coping mechanisms quickly enough, the thoughts don't have the chance to turn into feelings. You cut them off at the pass."

I nodded, trying to let the information sink in.

"Keep track of things that trigger you, learn some breathing techniques, and get yourself some tactile things to fidget with to calm you down. It takes practice, but eventually you can control your way of thinking. You practice by replacing thoughts. For example, instead of saying to yourself, 'I have to constantly yell out "be careful" to my children on the playground, because if I don't they will hurt themselves,' you can say to yourself, 'We have been to the playground many times before, and they haven't hurt themselves, and they probably won't.'"

"Right. Like, I hear you, but the one time I don't freak out is going to be the one time they break all their bones on the swing set," I said, taking a sip of my water.

"So tell yourself, 'My fears are not an indicator of future events and have no bearing on the outcome of this day. My brain is lying to me.'"

"Ohhhh, I love that. I'm actually going to use that," I replied.

"How does your husband feel about all of this?" he asked, grabbing his pen and notepad off the table.

I tried my hardest not to roll my eyes into the back of my skull. "My husband is never home. But he just thinks I'm crazy. He says I overreact to everything for no reason."

"I'd like you to bring him in," he said.

49

"DR. LEE, THIS IS COLIN, THE ONE I'VE BEEN GUSHING TO YOU about," I joked.

Colin rolled his eyes. "I bet," he said, shaking the doctor's hand.

"Have a seat," Dr. Lee said, gesturing toward the two empty chairs across from him.

"I appreciate you coming, Colin. I'm sure it took some convincing," he said.

"Not really. She asked me to come and I said okay."

Dr. Lee gave me an "I told you so" look, and I rolled my eyes and smiled.

"The reason I have asked Tiffany to bring you in is because I truly believe that an outside perspective can work wonders for a situation."

Colin suddenly looked uncomfortable. I'm not even sure he was aware there was a situation.

"Tiffany has some big feelings and has communicated to me that she has trouble expressing them."

"Okay," Colin said nervously. "Why does this feel like some sort of an intervention?"

Dr. Lee and I both spoke up at once. I decided to sit back and let him do the talking. It would probably be better coming from him. "This is nowhere near an intervention. I see this all the time in my patients, and it's imperative that a spouse is involved with the healing process."

"Healing?" Colin asked.

Dr. Lee paused. "Did you know that your wife has anxiety?" he asked point-blank.

"Um, well, I know she says she has it . . . anxiety. And I do notice her getting worked up about things often. But I don't know if it's actual anxiety or if she's just . . . tightly wound, you know?" Colin said.

"It is anxiety. And a rather severe case, I may add," Dr. Lee answered.

I wanted to cry. I had never felt more validated in my life.

"It's very real. When someone has anxiety, their brain tricks them into thinking they are in a life-or-death situation. They tend to go into survival mode. Perhaps that's why when you two are out in public together she seems frazzled. It's because in her mind, the world is a dangerous place and she is trying to keep her loved ones safe from it. Tiffany, let me ask you, what do you think of when you take the children for walks?"

I raised my eyebrows and let out a sigh. "Um . . . well, I try not to do that, take them for walks and stuff. It makes me feel like I'm going to explode, so I just don't do it. But if we do go, I'm thinking about cars whipping around the corner and running them over, or a dog darting out from someone's driveway and viciously attacking them. If they get too far ahead I picture someone pulling up next to them and yanking them into their car and taking them away. Depending on the weather that day, I tend to imagine getting struck by lightning. I saw a story of a woman who was walking her toddler around the block on a sunny day and BOOM, random-ass lightning zapped 'em both cuz they were holding hands. They lived, but like . . . still. Stuff like that."

Dr. Lee nodded.

"I just feel like our brains are like a filing cabinet, okay, and Colin somehow is able to pull out one file at a time. He looks at the file for a minute, tucks it back into its spot in the cabinet, and goes on his way. Meanwhile, my cabinet is flung wide open and someone's taking a fucking leaf blower to it."

"Tiffany," Colin scolded.

"I'm sorry, Dr. Lee, for cursing. But like, damn. I'm running around, snatching files out of the air all day, trying to make sense of them and put them back in the right spot. But no one sees the files. I just look like a big sweaty stressed-out bulldozer bounding through the house."

"Jesus," Colin said under his breath. It felt judgy.

"It's not like I want to feel those things, Colin. I can't help it. It's just how my brain works. You think I want to feel like this? This shit robs me of my joy every single moment of my life," I snapped, crossing my arms. "And I used to be able to just numb my way through the anxiety with drugs, and now . . . I mean, of all people, I think *you'd* understand."

"Tiffany," Dr. Lee said gently, "I don't think Colin was patronizing you. I think perhaps getting a glimpse inside your head may have been a bit surprising for him."

"Yeah, I mean. It sounds a bit extreme, to be honest. I don't think she's making it up or anything, but I feel like she puts a lot of this on herself," Colin said. "And I was an addict, too. But when I got sober, none of this shit came out."

I had to grip the chair to keep from stabbing Colin in the neck with my pen.

"That's why I'm glad you're here. You don't know what you don't know, and if you've never experienced this level of anxiety, it would be unfair to expect you to understand."

"Exactly, thank you," Colin replied. "Can I say something, Doctor?"

Dr. Lee nodded and gestured for him to continue.

"I didn't know that's how she felt. She never tells me that. She only yells at me for stuff that I'm not doing right. How am I supposed to know what she's thinking if she doesn't tell me?"

I didn't give the doctor a chance to respond. "Because every time I try to talk to you it's like talking to a box of cereal. Except a box of cereal is more fun because it's colorful and has puzzles and stuff." Okay, this is what I meant when I said I suck at arguing. "You seem really uninterested, Colin, like all the time—"

"It's because I am, Tiffany! Do you realize that the only words that ever come out of your mouth when you talk to me are hateful? You're either listing off the shit I'm failing at as a husband or bitching at me about how the things I *am* doing are wrong."

"Well, excuse me for wanting a little bit of assistance in raising our children. I have to tell you what to do because you are never freakin' there. Ever since you took over the company from George when he retired, you've been completely absent. How many times have I begged you to hire someone so you could spend a little time with us? You don't know anything that's going on inside that house. I bet you don't know that Kaiden can't wear certain fabrics anymore because he has some kind of fabric sensitivity going on and he only wants to wear shirts with pockets. You probably aren't aware that Addie got an A on her science test but needs to work on vocab. I've asked you six times to fix the hot water in the bathroom because it burns my nipples . . ."

"That explains why you haven't been showering."

"Perhaps I'd shower more if I knew there was a chance of me being touched every now and then."

"Okay, okay. Let's settle down for a moment," Dr. Lee said, raising his hand.

The room fell silent, with only the sounds of the clock ticking and me sucking in air remaining.

"I know you two are angry, but from a clinical perspective, that was an incredible breakthrough."

I'm gonna break through something here in a minute.

"Colin, let me ask you a question," Dr. Lee said, rubbing his chin. "Do you like working?"

I continued staring at the doctor. I was afraid that if I glanced over at my husband, I might karate-chop his Adam's apple.

"Do I like my job?" Colin asked.

"No, that's not what I asked. Do you like working?" he clarified.

"No, I hate it."

I shook my head. *No, you don't. You love it. You flip out of bed in the morning and skip to your truck, eager to get away from our chaos.*

"Why do you hate it?" he asked.

"I hate being in the sun all day and getting dirty. I hate that I'm gone all day. Some days I don't even see the kids."

I nodded hard with my arms still crossed.

"If you could, would you change places with your wife?" he asked.

"In a heartbeat," Colin replied.

I let out a loud snort. "What! No you wouldn't! No you freakin' wouldn't," I laughed.

"Yes I would, Tiffany, in a second. I'm not saying what you do is easy or anything, I'm just saying I'd much rather be with my family than working. You think I want to work so much? You think I like it? I have no choice. I have to work. This book and internet stuff is wonderful and it's bringing in money, which I'm grateful for, but it may go away in an instant. So I have to work. I have to get up at five thirty every morning and leave the house and my family behind, knowing I won't get back till seven or eight at night." He was becoming more animated, and leaned forward in his chair. "And when I do finally get home after a long-ass day, instead of being greeted with a smile or a hug, or God forbid some dinner, I'm greeted with dagger eyes. It's like I've already somehow ruined her day before I even set foot in the door."

His words struck me like lightning. I wanted to be offended and continue arguing my side of the case, but for the first time in our relationship, I got a glimpse inside his head . . . and it was actually quite sad.

"How does it make you feel, Tiffany, after hearing all that?" Dr. Lee asked thoughtfully.

I felt my chin begin to quiver. "It makes me feel sad. I feel kind of bad. For how I've been treating him. I thought he loved being away from us. I didn't know he would rather be home with us." I looked over at him and gave him an apologetic look. He reached for my hand and squeezed it.

"Communication in a relationship is vital. It's not 'recommended' or 'suggested'; it's crucial. Without it you have nothing. Acknowledging your part in these situations is a big step, Tiffany."

"I mean, there's more I could probably do," Colin said, riding the wave of optimism. "When I get home, I'm tired, and I kind of expect her to take care of the kids while I relax and stuff. I never really considered that she might need a break too," he said, turning to look at me.

"Tiffany," the doctor said. "In the spirit of acknowledging our parts in things, I want to say something to you, and I'm not sure you're going to like it."

Damn it, this had been going so well in my favor.

"Go ahead," I said, tensing up in preparation for what he was about to say. I hated constructive criticism, but I knew it was essential for growth. Blah, blah, blah.

"You have been using your anxiety as a shield to protect yourself from the truth, and it's time to stop," he said bluntly. If I were wearing pearls, I would have clutched them. "Earlier you said, in regard to your anxiety, 'This is just who I am. I can't help it.' In actuality what you are saying is 'I have anxiety so I will continue to lash out at you and you must take it without complaint because this is just who I am, and if you love me, then you must deal with it.'"

I stared straight ahead, absorbing what he'd just said.

"Tell me if this sounds better," he continued. "'I'm sorry if I seem on edge, honey, I am feeling anxious. It would really help me in these moments if you could *blank*.' Then you tell him exactly what you need from him in that moment. I can promise you that he will be more willing to help you if you are willing to help yourself. Go ahead and tell him now: What do you wish he would do in those moments of anxiousness?"

I turned to face Colin and pondered the doctor's question for a moment.

"You know, I just want to feel safe in what feels like a very unsafe world. If you could just hug me and tell me that I'm safe, and that while you don't necessarily understand how it feels, you recognize that it must be hard. Just love me through it. Validate me instead of calling me crazy. The danger feels so real to me in those moments, and I just want to know that I'm going to be okay."

Dr. Lee closed his eyes and nodded. "Do you think you can do that for her, Colin?"

"Absolutely. I never know what the hell to say or do when she gets upset and stuff, so that's actually super helpful."

"It's going to change everything, just you wait and see." Dr. Lee gave us a knowing smile, and nodded his head as if to say "bravo."

Colin and I rode home hand and hand, in silence. I think we were both afraid that if we said something it might ruin the momentum we had going. I spent the entire car ride thinking about all the times I'd allowed my anxiety to interfere with my marriage. I had been using it as a sword, cutting all the people around me repeatedly, and then getting angry at them for being upset that they were bleeding. I had a lot of work to do. We both did. But in that moment, I felt more connected to my husband than I had in years.

I should have known it was too good to be true.

50

PRESENT DAY

"YOU LOOK LIKE SHIT."

"It's nice to see you too, honey," Colin said, shutting the door behind him a few hours after I'd taken the kids to school. It was three days after he was supposed to come home. I couldn't even look him in his face; I was afraid to see this version of him. The sleep-deprived one with copious amounts of drugs coursing through his system. The one who had blown twelve thousand dollars of our savings in three days on God knows what.

I walked straight up the stairs into the playroom, a neutral place for us to gather. I hadn't spoken in any depth to him, but it went without saying that we were due for a conversation. Judging by the way he reluctantly followed me up the stairs, he already knew.

My heart pounded and my foot tapped wildly as he took a seat on the opposite end of the couch.

"What's up?" he mumbled as he lowered himself down.

I scoffed and shook my head. Anger coursed through me as I tried to find a way to communicate respectfully without lashing out. As angry as I was, I'd spent years learning to regulate my emotions and not be reactive. I needed him to remain open and honest, so approaching the situation with a level head would be crucial for me to get him to confide in me.

"Thank you for coming home," I said quietly. Our eyes met for the first time. There was no life behind his. He looked completely drained.

"Sorry it took so long," he replied, tears forming in his eyes.

"Well, since I changed the bank passwords and shut off the credit cards, I guess you had to."

He looked down. "Yeah, but that's not the only reason I came home."

I nodded. "How are you?"

"How do you think I am?" he retorted.

"I'd say you're probably feeling pretty good right about now. Did you use today?" I asked, staring down at my lap.

"No . . . Well, technically at like one in the morning, but not since I got on the plane."

"Listen, I need you to tell me the truth, okay. I'm telling you right now if you lie to me, I'll never forgive you, but if you tell the truth I'm willing to work through anything. I'm serious."

"Okay, what do you want to know?" he asked, wiping sweat from his forehead. I wasn't sure if it was the drugs or the fact that he was about to come clean about his little excursion, but either way, he looked gross.

"Did you hook up with anyone?" I asked point-blank.

"You asked me this before. No, dude. I would never."

I wanted to believe him, more than anything in the fucking world I wanted to believe him.

"I heard there were girls in the room, at least tell me if that's true. Even if you didn't hook up, were there girls?"

He shook his head. "Absolutely not. I promise you. It was just us guys and we were all so fucking paranoid we hardly left the room. I swear, Tiffany. I know I fucked up with the drugs, but I promise I would never cheat on you. Ever."

I nodded and wiped a tear from my cheek with the back of my hand.

"Can I ask you a question?" I asked, my voice shaky.

"Of course, you can ask me anything . . ."

"When you were looking down at those piles of drugs, did our kids' faces cross your mind at all?"

I saw his chin quiver, and he leaned forward and placed his face in his hands. His body shook with sobs. "No, I couldn't," he mumbled into his hands.

I nodded slowly and frowned. I couldn't wrap my brain around how he'd chosen drugs over our babies after a decade of sobriety. Never ever. How could he do this?

"Well, listen, things have to change. All of the trust I had for you is out the window, okay?"

"Geez, you really know how to kick a man when he's down."

I took a deep breath to center myself. "I don't give a shit. You spent over twelve thousand dollars of our family money and disappeared on a binge in Vegas. You deserve to be down and you deserve to be kicked. I'm not trying to make things worse here, I'm just beside my fucking self." He didn't reply, which was smart. "Now, I'm not saying you need to go to rehab, but you need to do something. You've fed the dragon, okay, you've given it all its power. If you're willing to get a sponsor and go to a meeting every day, we can work through this. Are you willing?" I asked, leaning down to meet his dropped gaze.

"Yes, Tiffany, of course. I'm willing to do anything to keep this family together. You guys mean more to me than anything in the world."

Part of me understood how powerful addiction truly is, but that part of me didn't show up in the playroom that day.

"Okay, is there anything else you need to tell me? Anything at all? This is it, Colin. If I find anything out from anyone else after this conversation, all bets are off."

"I've told you everything, I promise you, Tiffany."

I took a deep breath and exhaled sharply. I believed him. I had to believe him.

I stood up and made my way to a cushion next to him and wrapped my arms around him. My touch startled him, and once he realized what I was doing, he cried and hugged me tight. Feeling his body felt nice. For a little while there I was worried he might have been dead. But thankfully he was spared and given a second chance.

I should have held him a little tighter in that naive moment. It was the last "normal" moment I remember before life as I knew it was shattered into a thousand pieces.

51

COLIN WAS PASSED OUT ON THE COUCH. HUGGING HIM HAD
been nice, but letting him sleep in the bed we'd shared for the
last ten years felt too close. I wasn't ready. Part of me wondered
if I'd ever be ready. The other part of me couldn't imagine breaking up our family for one lousy weekend of ingesting booze and
pills and stabbing needles into veins and blowing thousands of
dollars and risking getting arrested or overdosing on a bathroom
floor . . .

God, it really did sound bad.

Would I want Colin to take me back if I'd relapsed? Of course.
But the difference was that I *hadn't*. For ten years I'd gone to
meetings, called my sponsor, and woken up every day telling myself "one day at a time." Every single day I'd worked my ass off
not just to stay sober, but to become the kind of parent I wanted
my kids to look up to. Meaning the one without a mug shot on
the internet (damn, it was too late for that). I wanted to be a parent who had learned from their mistakes and done the work nec-

essary to never, ever make them again. I desperately longed to be present for my kids, not spinning in another orbit chasing the next hit.

Colin had failed at that.

He hadn't just fucked things up with the kids, though. He'd fucked them up for himself. He was back at the starting line with about ten thousand marathons to run, and it wasn't going to be fun for him or for any of us.

I also wasn't sure I believed him. The kind of drugs Colin did didn't cost $12,000. He was either buying for his friends and random strangers, or something else was going on. Would it hurt anyone if I played private detective for just a teensy weensy bit? I guess not. If Colin was lying to me, I had to find out.

I looked over at Colin and saw his chest rising and falling steadily. He hadn't moved for a full hour, and he'd always been a good napper, so this was a positive sign. He wasn't going to wake up for another two hours at most. And the kids were going to be home in an hour, so my moment was now.

Colin had taken off his Apple watch and placed it on the side table. I stared at it. It was boring a hole into my skull.

You bought that watch, Tiffany, I told myself. *So, technically, it belongs to you.*

I tiptoed toward the side table and reached down. Grabbing the watch, I snuck out of the living room and into the kitchen. I put the watch on the counter and stared at it.

You can do this. You can do this.

I entered Colin's PIN and saw the photo of our kids on his backdrop. *Did you see that when you were calling your dealer?* I asked myself, then got furious all over again. Then I looked for the phone icon and pushed it. I closed it up and swiped toward his text messages.

My heart dropped to my stomach and continued beating there while I struggled to catch my breath.

Oh . . . my . . . God . . .

What I found on the watch was so much worse than I could've imagined. I grabbed my camera and recorded the messages. My breathing was heavy and labored. I just kept repeating *Oh my God* under my breath as I scrolled and scrolled and scrolled.

I bent down, thinking I was going to hyperventilate, then ran into another room, clutching my phone. I dialed a number I knew by heart.

"LANEY!" I whisper-yelled. "Don't ask any questions. Just pick the kids up at school and take them out for ice cream. Then take them back to your house and call me. I'll tell you if it's safe to bring them back here."

"You're freakin' me out," Laney responded.

"I know, I'm sorry, I promise everything is fine and I'll explain later. I'm safe. JUST DO IT."

"Okay, okay, okay . . ." she reluctantly agreed. I let out a sigh of relief. Truthfully I wasn't sure what was about to happen, but I knew my kids couldn't be here for it.

I tiptoed back into the playroom and saw Colin in the same position. He hadn't moved.

I shook him, hard. "Wake up, asshole," I said.

"Huh, what?" He gasped and looked around. He suddenly realized he was on the couch in the playroom, and I could see the relief wash over his face. Almost like everything that had happened was a dream and he was safe at home. He closed his eyes and lay back down, settling comfortably into the pillow.

I should have ripped the pillow away from him and beat his ass with it, because I would never allow him to be comfortable in this home ever again.

"I need your full attention."

"What?" he grumbled.

"I packed up some of your things. Get the fuck out of my house."

52

A WEEK LATER

"WHEN'S DADDY COMING HOME?" CHLOE ASKED, SHOVELING a spoonful of ice cream into her mouth.

"I'm not sure, baby, he's working at the moment."

"Daddy has a job?!"

I paused. She sounded so excited, so I guess I had to act like I was too. "Kind of! He's training to be the best daddy in the world and should be back soon!"

"But he already is the best daddy," Chloe said, seeming sad.

I clenched my jaw tight to keep from sharing my current opinion on that.

"Awww, honey, that's so sweet. He definitely is. Finish your ice cream and let's go watch a movie in my bed. I'll let you stay up late," I said, trying to distract them.

"Yay!" Kaiden and Chloe squealed in unison.

Colin had barely put up a fight once he'd been confronted

with his lies. He initially attempted to deny it, but once I began reciting the texts that had been forever burned into my memory back to him, he didn't have much to say. He didn't beg to stay or try to explain them away—which I appreciated at the time, because if I'd had to look at his deceitful face for a moment longer I might have ended up on *Dateline*.

I had reluctantly spoken to him a few times throughout the week and learned he was staying at his old sponsor's house and going to meetings. Unless he was excellent at covering it up, he'd stayed sober. As for me, I'd been letting Kaiden and Chloe sleep in my bed each night since he'd been gone. Addie was with her mom. Being alone in bed felt too strange, plus it felt safer having their little bodies directly next to me. I wasn't necessarily worried that he was going to do something dangerous like break in or anything, but then again I never thought he would do some of the things he did back in Vegas, and here we were . . .

"I love you, Mom," Chloe cooed.

"Me, too," Kaiden added.

Well, at least I had that. And it was *huge*.

As the three of us lay in bed watching the movie, my thoughts drifted to the predicament I'd found myself in. I was due to leave for a tour next week, and I still hadn't found a nanny to care for the kids in my absence. Having to leave my babies behind during a time like this made my stomach turn. At least if I was home I could protect them, answer their questions, and ensure that they weren't being traumatized by the fact their father had seemingly disappeared. But I was one of three headlining comics on a comedy tour, and couldn't quit in the middle of it. So much time, energy, and money had been put into the tour, and if I quit now, it would be disastrous.

"Lights out, kids," I said. It was getting late, and I was more tired than they were.

Was I too exhausted to sort my life—and this tour—out? I couldn't be. But, damn, it would have been so much easier to just give up.

A few days later a breaking news graphic popped up on the television in the background and caught my attention.

"Preparations under way for a potential category-five hurricane heading toward the East Coast!"

I sat down on the couch and turned up the volume.

"Hurricane Ian, a potential category-five hurricane, is on track to make landfall early next week, here's what you need to know."

Shit.

As the newscaster began listing off the ways to prepare, I let out a sigh and shook my head. Living in Florida, I was no stranger to hurricanes . . . Leaving my children behind in a hurricane with a stranger, however, was not something I was mentally prepared for.

I turned off the TV and realized I had a tough choice to make: stay home and ruin the tour, or allow Colin back into the house.

Damn it, I said to myself. *I gotta let the asshole back in.*

As long as he was sober, Colin was more than capable of caring for the kids while I was gone. He was a good dad, and except for Vegas, he'd always been. So I called Colin and asked, and he was more than willing. In fact, he was thrilled at the opportunity to spend time with them, and I'm sure the idea of sleeping in his old bed as opposed to his sponsor's couch was equally as exciting.

I, on the other hand, was dreading it.

.   .   .

"It's good to see you, Tiff." Colin smiled, carrying my suitcase out to the car for me.

"You too," I lied. I felt like being here was a privilege he didn't yet deserve, but selfishly I had no other choice.

"I'm gonna put the shutters up and bring the patio furniture inside. Don't worry about anything while you're gone, okay? I promise everything will be fine."

As much as I hated to admit it, his words were comforting.

"Thanks again for doing this. Please don't forget to give Chloe her medicine."

"I won't."

"There's a credit card for food and stuff on the counter. I'm gonna be tracking the transactions, so don't try—"

"Tiff, I promise, I won't use it for anything other than the kids and the house."

I nodded.

"Okay, well, I gotta go. Thanks again," I said, slamming the trunk shut.

"No problem." He paused briefly. "Can I have a hug?" He held out his arms.

"No," I replied before sitting in the driver's seat and shutting the door.

You will never get to touch me again.

53

—

"I *promise*," Colin responded. I could hear the annoyance in his voice. "Nothing has changed in the two hours since you last called."

I'd been a nervous wreck the entire trip, checking the local news and phoning or texting Colin constantly. Thankfully the hurricane hadn't hit my town directly, and apart from a few downed trees and power lines, everything was fine.

I sighed. "Okay, well, thank you. Please give the kids a big hug from their mom."

"I will. Now stop worrying."

Click.

As I heard the line go dead, I realized that something strange was happening to me. In the few days I'd been gone, I'd found myself looking forward to Colin's texts and actually wanting to speak with him. After our Friday-night show, I talked to him all the way from the venue to the hotel and for three hours after that. We went over everything and nothing. We even laughed. I was lonely, and after spending a decade with this person, he still felt like home to me. Which was confusing. I was simultaneously drawn to him and repulsed by him.

I might even say I missed him. I missed *us*.

When I got home from the tour, I scooped the kids up and hugged them so hard I thought I might break their backs.

"Mom, don't ever leave us again!" Chloe yelled.

Colin grunted. "Hey. Mom doesn't let you have ice cream every night. *I* do."

"Every night?!" It sounded incredible, but I didn't want them to get used to this.

"I'm kidding. But they did have ice cream for breakfast one day."

What I think might have been a smile formed on my mouth, and I quickly wiped it away. I didn't want Colin thinking I'd softened up.

He spoke up. "Hey, I don't want to interrupt whatever daydream you're having, but can I talk to you in private? No offense, kids."

Chloe stared daggers at Colin, but he shooed her away. We walked outside. I had no idea what he wanted to talk about, but I hoped it was something normal . . . like the kids' homework or that the bathroom sink was clogged again.

It was the opposite.

"Now, I don't want to lay this on you . . ." he said. "I know you just got back, but I've been thinking."

Oh no, oh no. I didn't know what to expect, but whatever was about to come out of his mouth sounded dramatic.

"Um, would you consider marriage counseling, Tiff? Just to see if there's a way to save this. I don't want to lose you, and being in this house again with the kids has made me realize there's nothing in the world I want more than to have this family together."

I felt the blood drain from my face. A week ago I wanted him to rot in hell, and now I was half considering the ludicrous idea that I might try to make this work.

Or was I?

It's a mistake, I told myself. *A colossal, life-changing, self-destructive mistake. You're going to get hurt, and this time it will be worse than the first time.*

But . . . what if things were different?

I suddenly remembered the good times. I thought of the joy in our kids' voices when they heard Colin come home. I thought of the day we brought Kaiden home from the hospital, and the time Chloe learned how to ride a bike. I thought of dancing around the house to Kidz Bop, and that time we saw *Frozen II* and couldn't stop singing the songs on the way home.

"Um, sure. We can find someone. I . . . ." My voice trailed off. I didn't want him to know how happy I was to hear what he'd said.

"Oh, good," he answered. And I opened my arms and let him come in for a hug.

I'm not sure if it was the jet lag, the loneliness, or the desperate need for dopamine, but for some reason, instead of sending him back to his sponsor's that night, I let him stay. In my bed. Naked. And I was naked too.

You get what I'm saying.

Between elation and hope and a little bit of ecstacy, I couldn't stop wondering . . . *What the hell is wrong with me?*

The following morning I woke up and was instantly overwhelmed with regret. It reminded me of the days I used to get blackout drunk, make stupid decisions, and feel like garbage the next morning. Except I was stone-cold sober. I'd allowed Colin back in—figuratively and literally—and I was both shocked and disappointed with myself for doing so.

His actions were reprehensible, and he didn't deserve to touch me. But I'd let him. Did that make me foolish and weak? At the time, I truly believed I was.

So I acted on that self-loathing.

"Colin," I said over coffee that morning, after I'd taken the kids to school. "Why don't you stay?"

"Like, *stay* stay?" He looked shocked, with just the teeniest bit of joy.

"Yes," I answered. "I'm sure."

I'd said it with determination. Was I convincing him, or myself?

54

"YOU SURE THIS IS THE RIGHT MOVE? I MEAN, MY HUSBAND IS still in the doghouse with me. You're acting like you're trying to be Betty Crocker in the kitchen and a porn star in the bedroom."

I was getting lunch with Liz, and she was skeptical of my home situation. Understandably so. In the weeks after my tour, I'd begun chasing Colin's attention and affection like it was a drug. I stopped eating, started tanning, and allowed him to do whatever he wanted with me sexually, whenever he wanted to. I needed his validation, I needed him to choose me. I needed to prove to myself that I was enough for him. And we'd become closer than ever.

"I'm *sure*. Stop worrying about me." I reapplied my lipstick and smoothed out my shirt. I'd lost ten pounds in a month. Take that, Vegas.

"I'm not going to interfere," she answered. "But I'm a little worried about you."

"I have to at least try to make this work, Liz, for the kids. That way in the future when they ask, I can honestly tell them I tried everything."

She nodded, but I knew she didn't understand. Neither did the rest of my friend group. They teetered the line between trying to support me and trying to save me from more heartache.

"So, how's counseling?"

I was glad she asked. Even though I doubted her true feelings, it was a relief to talk about it. "Well, it sounds weird, but we've opened up to each other more than we ever have. I've left each appointment on cloud nine, feeling hopeful for the future."

"Nice!"

I couldn't tell if that was sarcasm or empathy. "I mean, since we've been seeing someone, Colin's been more affectionate, loving, and complimentary than he was the previous ten years combined. And he's working so hard on his recovery."

"That's amazing. And I hope it stays that way."

"Me too," I mumbled, and I hoped I'd hidden the fear in my voice.

"Earth to Colin?!" I said, waving my hand in front of his face. He was on the couch staring at his phone, which I wanted to yank out of his hands and toss out the window. I'd said his name four times before he finally noticed.

"Oh, yeah, sorry. I was just . . ."

"Never mind." I stormed out of the room.

It was day four after therapy. I should have expected this.

For the past few months, I'd noticed the windows of time in which he was my "dream husband" had become smaller and smaller after couples therapy. We'd have an amazing session, and for the next two days we'd sit down together and communicate and be loving and affectionate. But by day four he'd regress back to the aloof, quiet, seemingly uninterested version of himself that I'd known for years. It was almost like at first he was so unbelievably grateful to have his family back that he'd do whatever it took to make me happy. Then eventually he'd get comfortable and stop making an effort.

"Okay, not never mind," I said, turning around and walking back to the couch. "I need to talk about something."

"I'm listening." Colin put down his phone and acted like he was paying attention.

"I know we went over this during our last session, but I need to go over it again. You know how in therapy I can ask you any question—I mean, any time I feel triggered?"

"Yup."

"Well, for probably five months you were totally on board. You'd gladly share anything I wanted to know."

"Okay."

"But now . . . you just seem annoyed."

Colin scrunched up his face. "Babe. If we're talking about Vegas again, I guess I am. I just don't know why you still don't trust me. I mean, when is this going to stop?"

I felt my face turn red. "You mean, when am I going to get over the fact that you disappeared for three days, blew half our savings, and broke our vows? Like, 'Hey babe, I know I destroyed your image of marriage and ability to trust another human being ever again, but it's all good. I'm back. So let's watch Netflix and act like nothing happened.'"

Colin shifted in his seat and leaned forward. He looked more pissed than I'd ever seen him. "Tiffany, it's NOT like that. I know what I did. I said I'm sorry. I am doing my hardest to make it up to you. But . . . it's been six months and you're still furious at me half the time. The other half of the time you're talking about dieting or your spray tan."

That was a low blow.

"I'm trying my best too. It isn't fucking easy. I'm scared to trust again. It no longer comes naturally. I'm terrified I'm going to look stupid again, more stupid than I already do for sticking by your side through this shit instead of leaving."

"I'M YOUR HUSBAND AND I LOVE YOU." Colin had stood up at this point. Was he threatening me? Or about to walk out? Either way, I was jonesing for a fight, so I wanted him to bring it on.

"It's not enough, Colin. I need you to listen."

"I *do* listen, and I *do* trust you," he fumed. "Why can't you learn to trust *me*? I've said I'm sorry. I just don't know what else I can do."

"This is not about you! It's about me for once!"

We were both standing up, face-to-face. "For once? It's always about you. Your feelings, your book, your Instagram, your anxiety . . ."

"How dare you?" I backed up, afraid I might do something stupid. I was livid. "My anxiety almost killed me. I learned to work through it, and now I'm finally learning to work through your betrayal. But that's not good enough for you. You feel like I should be over it by now, and I feel like I'm just getting started."

That got him. Colin sat back down and crossed his arms.

"I'm sorry. I should not use your anxiety against you. Nor should you use my relapse against me."

Point for Colin. I nodded.

"But I just feel like I'm going to spend the rest of my life trying to convince you I'm doing the right thing, and you're never going to believe me."

For someone who usually spoke about two words an hour, he was making good sense. The truth was, I wasn't sure I *could* ever trust him again. In a lot of ways, his words were the writing on the wall.

"The person you are asking me to be is not who I am, Tiffany."

I couldn't speak, but my thoughts were clear in my head: My husband and I were fighting an uphill battle, and even if we did make it to the top, I wasn't sure he was the one I wanted standing up there with me.

I started to tear up. "I'm not asking for much. I'm just asking you to communicate more, ask me how my day was, be more present. I just want to feel like you want me."

"I do want you! But it's like, the person you keep saying you want me to be—this outgoing, funny, talkative, affectionate-ass dude—it's not me. It will never be me. It's like you're trying to change the chemical makeup of my brain. I'm sorry I'm not enough for you, and honestly I don't think I ever will be."

I nodded, and the tears began to fall. I was devastated but my body felt a sense of relief. The air became more breathable. I looked at Colin and saw that he felt the same release. Thank God one of us had said it. He was right. I'd known deep down for years that we weren't compatible. There was always more I wished he'd say, more I wished he'd do. I couldn't spend the rest of my life teaching someone how to treat me, and it wasn't fair to him to go through life always feeling less than, or like what he had to offer wasn't good enough.

It was me who spoke first.

"So, what are we going to do?"

55

THE MEDIATOR BUSTLED INTO THE ROOM CLUTCHING A brown folder stuffed full of papers. She gave us a quick smile and turned to shut the office door. I glanced at the side of Colin's face in search of a hint as to what he was thinking. Was he sad about this? Was he excited that it was happening? Was he going to jump up and drop to his knees in tears, pleading that we give this some more thought before making it official?

As usual, his blank expression provided no answers.

"All right. How are we today?" she asked, taking a seat in front of us and flipping open the folder.

"Good," Colin replied, flashing a quick smile. It was his fake smile, the one I'd seen millions of times. Did that mean he *wasn't* good? Was he having second thoughts? We should have discussed this more. Maybe we'd made this decision a little too fast. After all, we'd just begun the divorce process two weeks ago.

I felt Colin's and the mediator's eyes on me and realized it was my turn to respond. "Great!" I blurted out, forcing a smile. I wasn't great at all. I wasn't even here . . . in this room. My body was, but my mind was back at our first apartment the day we moved in, when excitement was bursting from every pore in our bodies. He'd scooped me up into his arms and swung me around in circles, squeezing so tightly I was afraid he might hurt the baby I had inside me. That day was the first day of our new life, and it was full of so much hope and happiness.

"Great, I'm just gonna have you confirm some information, and then we'll send you on your way," she explained, bringing her attention back down to the paperwork in front of her. I followed her gaze, afraid to look over at Colin. This was all so strange.

"You have three children, correct?" she asked, peering at Colin over the brim of her glasses.

He cleared his throat and adjusted in his seat. "Yes."

"And you have two children, correct?" she asked me.

"Three," I corrected. "Well, technically, two that came out of my body, but I count my bonus daughter also, since I've been with her since she was tiny."

"Okay, yeah. Gotcha. So, we don't actually count your stepdaughter, because technically after the judge signs off on all this, you no longer have any rights to her."

I swallowed down the lump in my throat and looked over at Colin, expecting him to come to my defense. He stared down at his hands, picking at one of his fingernails. Addie had always been one of my children. Three toothbrushes, three bedrooms, three sets of presents Christmas morning, three snacks from the gas station anytime I stopped at one. Three of everything as long as I'd been a mother. I'm not sure why it never dawned on me that from now on I'd be considered a mother of . . . just two.

"Okay, but I still get to be a part of her life, right? Like, I still have the right to see her and spend time with her and stuff, right?"

"Unfortunately, technically, according to the law—"

"Yes," Colin interrupted, "yes, of course. You've been there for everything, all her life. You still get to be a part of her life. It's all she's known." He stared into my eyes with sincerity, and I could tell he meant it. I relaxed my shoulders and let out a silent sigh.

The mediator gestured to him. "Of course, if Colin and the biological mother are okay with that arrangement, that's perfectly fine. Now, legally, if they change their minds, unfortunately, there's nothing we can do about that." She licked her finger and continued flicking through the papers.

I felt my chin begin to quiver. *Don't be a little bitch, Tiffany. This is what you wanted. This is the right decision. Don't second-guess yourself.*

I smiled and nodded in response.

"Okay, and what is the plan for custody? Did you fill out the paperwork?"

Colin slid the paper across the desk, and she picked it up to examine it. "We are going to do a two/three plan, like days on days off. At least I think that's what we're doing."

I nodded and laughed. "Yes, I don't think I'd survive if we did a one week on, one week off." It wasn't a real laugh; there was nothing funny about it. The idea of going more than a day without seeing my kids made me want to die.

She continued asking questions about assets and finances, and my eyes glazed over. I heard her and Colin murmuring in the distance about alimony and child support, but I couldn't focus because it all sounded so foreign to me. Colin had always handled the "business" side of things. I had no clue what escrow or equity meant, and, honestly, I didn't care. I knew I *should* care, but I couldn't bring myself to. I'd spent all my energy on other things. The future, the kids, what this meant for their mental health. Caring about whether I was doing the right thing or royally screwing up my family. Caring about how I was going to survive financially when my job was to make people laugh on the internet. I hadn't felt funny in a long time. Caring about my recovery—and Colin's, for that matter. Relapsing at a time like this seemed like a distinct possibility.

I hadn't asked for any of this, and, frankly, it seemed really unfair. The things that led us here were not my choice.

Except they kind of were. After all the counseling we did over months, I knew we couldn't make it anymore. Maybe we were never destined to be. But that didn't matter. After the hurricane, I knew we could co-parent, and maybe—just maybe—that's all I needed.

"As you know, Florida is a no-fault state," she said, and I tuned back out. I nodded along as she outlined the terms of the agreement, and I understood that by signing, I was agreeing to them.

"All right, if each of you could sign at the bottom, I'll get this sent over to the judge ASAP."

I let out a sigh and nodded slowly, reaching for the pen. I looked over at Colin, studying his face one last time, hoping to find an inkling that he wasn't ready, or didn't want this.

"You sure you wanna do this?" he asked. It reminded me of the day of our wedding when he'd asked me the same thing. Much like that day, I wasn't sure . . .

Thinking about the past was pointless. So was remembering our wedding, our first apartment, or all the other good times. I refused to regret how quickly we'd rushed in, trying so hard to prove everyone wrong. I had to focus on reality. On the things that had happened, that I'd tried my hardest to work through, and that had gotten us to this place. The things that tore me to shreds and left me questioning my entire existence. Those were the things that mattered, those were the things that were *real*. I couldn't believe we were here, that this was what my reality had become.

"I'm sure," I replied before scribbling my signature on the dotted line.

56

"IS THIS YOUR HUSBAND?" THE EMAIL SUBJECT LINE SAID. I scrolled down and saw a photo of Colin. He was sitting directly across from a blonde at a local restaurant, and all I could see of her was the back of her head.

I rolled my eyes and turned off my phone. "He's not my husband anymore," I wanted to reply, but after four months, I still hadn't felt ready to tell the world. I didn't want the opinions of thousands of strangers, and I certainly didn't want to share anything on social media that could get back to the kids one day. They were already trying their best to navigate the split homes, and I didn't want to add to their trauma.

My mental state was like glass the first few weeks following the divorce. It didn't take much for me to fall apart completely at a moment's notice. In the beginning, the feelings of anguish, rage, jealousy, sadness, and loneliness seemed to consume me. Some days I'd find a way to heal, whether it was through talking with my friends or my sponsor, or just doing some good old-fashioned inner-child work. But just as I'd start to feel optimistic and hopeful again, I'd run into Colin at the Walgreens on the corner. Or, rather, see him with some other woman in an email sent by a total stranger.

Unfortunately, divorcing someone you've created children with is like having that Walgreens feeling every two to three days. You don't get a break from it, you don't have time to heal, and you don't have enough solitude to escape from it and learn who you are away from the place that hurt you. You're required to revisit that place every two days.

Transferring the children back and forth was surreal. It was so strange to go from talking to someone all day every day for ten years to going days at a time without hearing their voice. I had no clue what he did over at his house and he had no clue what I did at mine. For all I knew, he was having orgies and keg parties when he didn't have the kids.

On the nights I didn't have them, I roamed the hallways like a ghost, lost and searching for a purpose. Coming home to a silent house after a decade of laughter and Disney songs playing all hours of the day was jarring and painful. The silence was deafening, and I spent many nights crying on their empty beds.

I'd made a career out of making people laugh, and it felt as if all the humor had been sucked right out of my body with a vacuum.

"Mom! Put down your phone!" Kaiden's voice jarred me from my thoughts, and for a split second I forgot about Colin and the girl at the restaurant.

"Okay, party animals! Get your stuff, it's bouncy time!" I yelled, a little too happily, as I jumped up and grabbed my purse.

It was his ninth birthday, and it would be the first time we'd be together as a "family" since we'd signed the divorce papers.

You can do this, Tiff, I told myself. *It's just a birthday party.*

When we entered the bounce house place, something caught my eye. Or rather, someone. There was a beautiful girl with hot pink leggings and a white crop top checking in two little girls at the front desk. Something about her looked familiar, but I couldn't put my finger on it. I knew whenever Colin arrived he'd be attracted to her, and it was so strange not being able to say anything about it. I couldn't. He wasn't my husband and could stare at whoever's big boobies all he wanted.

Over the course of the next hour, that's exactly what he did.

"What is he doing, undressing her with his eyes?" Liz asked as I spotted Chloe sprinting from one bouncy slide to another.

"Maybe he's just looking at that ice cream she just got from the snack bar."

"Yeah," Liz laughed. "Two huge, round scoops of it."

Colin kept stealing glances at her. She was hard for me to miss, too. Everywhere I turned, there she was. I asked myself why I was so jealous. Maybe because it was the first time I'd gotten to hang out with Colin since the divorce and hoped he'd be more focused on his family than the blond supermodel bouncing all around us?

It wasn't until Elyse and Amber arrived at the party that I knew something was up.

"Is that girl here for the party?" Elyse asked, pointing to the blond woman in hot pink leggings who'd been circling the party like a shark and who had just left one of the bounce houses.

Must be nice to be young and spry and not piss your pants each time you rebound on the trampoline, I thought.

"No, dude, but she's very much all up in our business, right?" I responded. "Like, she's always around."

Amber and Elyse exchanged worried glances.

"What?" I asked, my heart starting to race.

Amber looked at me and I could have sworn I saw pity in her face. "Tiffany . . . I think that's the girl who comments on all of his Instagram posts."

"Instag— He has Instagram? Wait, and that girl right there comments on it? They know each other?" I pointed to Pink Pants.

Amber nodded nervously.

Suddenly everything clicked. The sneaky glances, the flirty smiles, the fact that she was hovering. And I knew that haircut. It was the woman from the restaurant photo! She wasn't a random stranger at all . . . She was here for my ex-husband.

57

___

MY HEART HAMMERED IN MY CHEST AS I MARCHED UP TO Colin.

"Are you going to invite her up for cake, or are you two going to just keep pretending you don't know each other?" I asked, my voice shaking with rage.

Of course I had no right to be angry. Colin was a grown, single man. I suppose it was the fact that these two idiots were pretending they didn't know each other, trying to be sneaky and secretive, that pissed me off.

I was sick of being made to look foolish by being in the dark.

"What the hell are you talking about, Tiffany?" he asked, running both hands down his face in frustration.

"Stop. Let's not do this. I'm not stupid, okay? If you couldn't wait two hours without seeing your girlfriend, you could have just told me she was coming. The fact that she's been sneaking around our kid's party for an hour pretending not to know anyone—as if she just happened to be a stranger here with her kids at the same time as us—it's just gross."

He sighed. "Tiffany, it's not even like that. I didn't want to upset you—"

"Wellll, you did. Not because I'm jealous, but because once again you've tried to make me look stupid. You two planned this. You should have just been honest. And what kind of woman does that? At our child's birthday party? It's fucked up, and now this memory is tarnished forever. She's in the back of all the fucking party pictures."

"Tiffany, I'm sorry."

"I don't give a shit," I said, walking away.

I actually did give a shit . . . a huge one. This woman was perfect—she was everything I'm not. It had been four months since the divorce, and while I'd been crying and questioning my worth and planning birthday parties and paying alimony and trying to survive, he was be-bopping around town with a Disney princess. Where were his consequences? When did he get to suffer? He was the one who fucked up, not me, so why the hell was I the one in constant pain?

This man was my husband four months ago, and somehow he'd already gotten over me and moved on to a much younger, much more beautiful woman. I couldn't even fathom being with anyone else. He must not have loved me as much as I'd thought.

Colin followed me and tapped on my shoulder. "Can we just not fight here? At our son's party? I know I have a lot of explaining to do, but we have to be here for Kaiden."

I closed my eyes. As always, he was the peacemaker. The one who could put a fire extinguisher on my anxiety and defensiveness and get me to back the hell off. The one whose solution to our hugely unexpected pregnancy was to settle down, to make it right. The one who could say "Sure, whatever you want, babe" and make even my stupidest ideas sound doable. He was right. We had to be here for Kaiden. We had to stop fighting.

"I know, Colin. I'm sorry. Let's just try to be the best parents we can be."

"Thank you, Tiff," he said, smiling.

"And when you have a chance, introduce me to the *Baywatch* chick, okay?"

"I saw Dad and Becca kissing."

"Do I have to call her Mom?"

For the next few weeks, each time one of my children brought up the name of either of them, it was like a sharp knife blade into my heart. Yet I couldn't flinch, I couldn't waver, I had to smile and seem unbothered in order to not further traumatize the children, who didn't ask for any of this.

Now when they spent time with their father, there was a new woman and her two children there. It had barely been a month since the party and I'd received updates that she was "at Dad's every day and they even got a dog."

Of course they got a dog.

I felt like checking myself into a mental institution. The lonely nights, the images in my mind of Colin and another woman together, the fact that I was over here in survival mode while he got to live his best life . . . it was too much for me to handle.

I had to take my life back, and that would start with baby steps.

The right side of the driveway had always been my side. I'd always squeezed my car in next to Colin's truck, my two right tires practically in the grass. On a random Wednesday afternoon, after picking up some groceries, I pulled into my driveway, and instead of moving the car toward the right, I stayed the course. Smack dab in the center. As I slowed the car to a stop, I noticed my tires weren't edging onto the grass.

I chuckled to myself as I turned down the Lizzo song I was listening to and put the car in park.

"Yes, bitch, that's more like it."

It was a small adjustment but somehow made me feel powerful. This was *my* driveway, in front of *my* house.

I could do anything I wanted . . .

A sense of independence rose from within me, and I marched into the house with conviction.

"This is my house, and I can decorate it however the hell I want now," I said to no one.

Then I went from room to room pulling down photos and wooden signs about "Love" and "Gathering" down from the walls. I'd originally chosen a farmhouse theme for the house because I thought that's what all the suburban wives were meant to have. Personally, it had always been too much white and beige for my liking, but I'd wanted to fit in with the rest of the ladies in the neighborhood.

"Time for a change! Buh-bye, Joanna Gaines."

That afternoon, I drove to the paint store and stocked up. Then I went into my garage and pulled out a box with a label that read "Witchy Stuff." The next day, I painted the walls and hung up my crystal displays and hand-painted art. Colin hated incense, so I lit up a stick, letting it burn to ash. Then I lit another one. Within two days, my bedroom was purple and black, and the house felt like mine. I even used a hammer and nails to hang things all by myself without a man's help—something I never thought I could do.

That started happening a lot, in fact, finding out I could do more than I thought I was capable of. It sounds silly, but pulling the garbage cans to the end of the driveway made me feel like a boss-ass bitch. "I don't need no man," I'd whisper to myself as I hobbled with the heavy trash can over the bricks of the driveway.

I was making progress, and I was proud.

Soon, I realized it was time to make my mind as orderly, efficient, and true-to-me as my house. I'd been swinging dangerously between stubbornly determined strength and paralyzing heartache, and I wanted to get well.

Really well. On my own terms.

"Dad lets us stay up till nine!" Kaiden yelled, squeezing his Capri-Sun.

Well, your dad sucks balls, I wanted to reply, but thanks to the help of a betrayal trauma therapist I'd started seeing, I knew exactly how to respond.

"That's okay! Here your bedtime is eight thirty."

"But why?! Dad lets us stay up extra," he whined. *"Pleeeease?"*

I paused to compose myself. "Okay, well, I'll talk to your dad"—*and whoop his ass*—"and we'll see if we can come to some kind of compromise. Okay?"

"Okay, but I still like Dad's house better."

"Me too!" Chloe chimed in. "When Becca brushes my hair she does it soft. You do it like you're ripping it out of my head!"

A month ago that comment would have sent me to a mental facility. But now I was able to smile and nod and almost mean it.

Thanks to trauma therapy, my mind was clearer, and reality didn't seem so distorted or terrible. Each week my therapist and I would meet, and she'd help me sort out my thoughts, identifying the rational ones and helping me discard the rest. Since Vegas, I hadn't been in a place where I could trust my own thoughts and feelings, and I no longer knew what was real and what was made up in my head. I'd started running everything by my friends because the decision fatigue had become overwhelming.

My life had been shaken up like a snow globe, but therapy helped me navigate the mess.

I could now answer my kids' questions and tell them how happy I was for their dad without sneaking into the bathroom and having a silent cry. Getting emails and inbox messages and comments under videos asking where my husband was, or saying things like "We always knew he would leave for someone hotter" no longer sent me into a spiral of depression. I'd even met Becca, and I liked her, pink pants aside.

When life threw the worst it had at me, when I was at my lowest, it was my friends who saved me. Even when I wanted to be alone, my friends insisted on coming and sitting with me. Elyse would come and have sleepovers so that I wouldn't be alone. I couldn't make decisions on my own at all. I had to call a friend to help me know what to eat for dinner. But my friends taking those calls and showing up for me is what got me through. It's what kept me strong in my sobriety even when my life was falling apart.

I couldn't take any of this for granted. So many of my role models in recovery hadn't had the same luck.

Life was getting better. I may have still been a mess at times, but at least I was a clean mess.

58

THE WHEELS TOUCHED DOWN IN VEGAS AND LIZ SQUEEZED my leg. She probably knew what I was thinking, which was *What the hell am I doing here?* I couldn't avoid thinking about that moment when Colin landed in Vegas a year and a half before. I'd sworn I'd never set foot in this city in my life. And here I was with my friends, about to walk a red carpet and host an awards show. Walking a red carpet was on my bucket list, but revisiting the scene of my husband's shenanigans definitely wasn't.

I was instantly overwhelmed by the bright lights and loud sounds that the city had to offer. There were triggers everywhere. People partying, drinks clinking. We had to pass through the windowless casino to get to our room. Even though it was midday, the casino was full of scantily clad women and it could just have easily been midnight.

I could see how seductive this city could be to anyone, especially an addict.

"You ready to do this?" Amber asked a few hours later, adjusting the strap of my $400 sparkly gold dress. It was way more than I could afford, but Liz had convinced me it was worth the splurge, given the circumstances.

I smiled and nodded.

"You're amazing, and we are so freakin' proud of you," Elyse said, wiping her tears with a handkerchief.

I rolled my eyes and laughed. "Always so emotional."

"You're gonna kill it, bitch, and it's going to be amazing," Liz said, grabbing my shoulders and shaking them.

"Thank you." I took a deep breath. "And honestly, thank you so much for coming. I know it wasn't easy, for any of us, to come here. I don't think I could have made the trip without your support."

"All right, Tiff, you're on," the director said, handing me a microphone.

"We'll be out there cheering obnoxiously loud for you." Liz smiled, and the rest of the girls nodded and waved.

I took a deep breath and composed myself before stepping out onto the stage. The announcer's voice boomed throughout the theater: "Everybody welcome your host, Tiiiifffany Jenkins!"

The crowd erupted in cheers, and I waved and laughed, taking center stage.

"Hi, everybody! I'm Tiffany Jenkins . . . like the guy just said."

A few chuckles escaped the crowd.

I paused for a moment and glanced over at my friends in the front row, who had been through so much with me over the past year. We were all individually working through the repercussions of Vegas. And although some of our marriages had fallen apart in the aftermath, the one thing that had remained constant was our friendship.

"I just want to say one thing before we get started tonight," I said, flashing my friends a smile. "Tonight is incredibly special to so many of us. Getting to celebrate all of the content creators who spread so much joy, and handing out awards for all the positivity they've spread is a dream come true. But I almost turned down the offer to host the show."

I could see the fear in the director's eye as I went off-script, but I didn't care.

"I almost said no because Vegas has a lot of bad juju for me. It's all about drinking and partying here, and I've worked so hard to stay clean. And then about a year ago some pretty tragic things happened to my friends and me. Our lives were flipped upside down after some people close to us took a trip to Vegas. You know how they say 'What happens in Vegas stays in Vegas'?" Everyone laughed. "Well, for someone very close to me, it didn't stay that time. But I've decided what better way to move forward than stepping out of my comfort zone and flying here. Standing here, I realize how much power we all have to bring positivity to even the darkest of places. We are so much more resilient than we realize. Life has a way of throwing curveballs at you. Sometimes those curveballs are on fire, too. But if you surround yourself with good people and remember that you're stronger than you fucking think you are, you can make it through anything."

I paused an extra beat for the full effect.

"All of that is to say . . . WELCOME TO VEGAS, BABY! It's an honor to be here."

ACKNOWLEDGMENTS

—

Writing this book—much like the life that it's written about—has been a journey. I am so grateful to have had the help of so many along the way. I would love to acknowledge some of those that were behind the scenes as I traversed the undertaking of my second book.

To Donna Loffredo, my editor at Random House, for answering all of my questions and really guiding me through the whole process of writing this book (and the many shapes it has taken over the years). I couldn't have done it without you.

To my editor, Sarah Durand, whose expertise not only helped in the technical process of editing, but whose guidance really helped hone my story into a work to be proud of.

To my friends and family, who stood by my side and helped nurture a space where I could tell my story and put to words the events that shaped these years of my life.

To everyone who has read my first book and shared their positivity. I am overwhelmed with joy hearing about how the stories of my life have helped others find the strength to move on to the next chapter of their lives.

Lastly, to my beautiful children. They give me reason to find strength and ground myself as my life's story contiunes to unfold. They are EVERYTHING.

ABOUT THE AUTHOR

TIFFANY JENKINS is the bestselling author of *High Achiever*. She uses her platform (@jugglingthejenkins) to help and inspire others who are struggling with motherhood, mental health, and addiction, as well as those who just need a good laugh. She speaks frequently about addiction and recovery. She lives with her family in Sarasota, Florida.